THE SOCK OBSESSION

THE SOCK OBSESSION

Supercool Socks to Knit and Show Off

Summer Lee

Author of *The Sock Project*

Abrams, New York

CONTENTS

Abbreviations

beg Beginning
CC Contrasting color(s)
CN Cable needle
CO Cast on
cont Continue
dec Decrease
inc Increase
k Knit
k2tog Knit two stitches together
kfb Knit into the front and back of the same stitch
ktbl Knit through the back loop
m Marker
m1l Make one new stitch (left)
m1r Make one new stitch (right)
MC Main Color
p Purl
p2tog Purl two stitches together
pm Place marker
ptbl Purl through the back loop
rnd Round
sl Slip
ssk Slip, slip, knit
st Stitch
wyib With yarn in back
wyif With yarn in front

LES TIGRES
Heureux
PREMIUM
TROPICAL STRENGTH RUM
TRIPLE DISTILLED

Introduction

I grew up in a rural Oklahoma town of roughly four hundred people and ten thousand cows. My days were spent wandering along railroad tracks, swimming in ditch water, climbing trees, reading *Baby-Sitters Club* books, and spying on my neighbors, recording their comings and goings in a notebook. Sometimes I joined up with other feral children, the dirty lot of us forming a loose pack as we loped around town on imaginary quests. But often I was alone, as I preferred to be, telling myself stories and plotting intricate and fantastical things to make.

Living my best small-town life

I had no crafting skills to speak of as a child. I didn't know how to knit or crochet, embroider or sew, paint or draw. But that didn't stop me from constantly *creating*. I made little people out of eggshells, complete with egg-people houses made of shoeboxes. I made gnomes out of toilet paper tubes. (And did I wait until a roll of toilet paper was finished before absconding with the cardboard tube? I did NOT. I unwound six rolls and left a mountainous pile of toilet paper on the bathroom counter for the next person to deal with.)

As a perpetually broke young adult still obsessed with the act of creation, I wanted to learn to knit so I could save money on my wardrobe (LOLOLOL!). The Internet had really picked up steam by then, and here were all these virtual grandmothers showing me the way via my cracked computer screen. I learned my knit stitch and my purl stitch, and then I produced the world's ugliest scarf. Looking at it, I was confused and, frankly, pissed off. Why, *why* was it so hideous? There were holes, dropped stitches, twisted stitches, and edges that creeped in and then crept right back out. It was not the squishy, supple scarf I had pictured in my head. It was an itchy, maroon tentacle that would choke me and give me a rash.

Hanging out with fellow sock knitters in Arkansas

Usually, I dropped a craft if I wasn't good at it (my closets were a graveyard of abandoned ambitions). Picking things up and then discarding them was the theme of my young adulthood. But knitting had rooted itself somewhere in my rib cage, and despite this failure I kept at it.

Twenty years later, knitting, miraculously, is my career, my life's work, and the obsession that keeps me awake at night, dreaming up new designs, new ideas to try out, and new color combinations to experiment with.

And not just any knitting, but sock knitting specifically. My journey started with that one ugly maroon scarf and has culminated in an entire five-drawer dresser filled with colorful hand-knit socks.

I found my own book in a bookstore!

In my first book, *The Sock Project*, I shared the ins and outs of sock knitting: how to make them, how to modify them, and how to fill a sock drawer with basics, as well as techniques like colorwork, stripes, fades, lace, cables, and texture.

In this book, we're going deeper into our shared obsession with all things sock knitting. I'll take you around the world, drawing inspiration from our ancestral traditions. We'll explore more modern design ideas, like how experimenting with color can free you from the shackles of what is right and wrong. I'll give you a cache of beloved everyday socks that can be knit time and again when you need something soothing and practical on the needles. We'll dive into the art of whimsical stranded knitting, because everyone needs a pair of lobster socks in their wardrobe. Finally, I'll really let loose and give you a curated collection of my signature socks—my favorite five patterns that most represent the colorful, edgy, cheerful ethos I've been cultivating since I first picked up a pair of teeny little needles and began knitting socks.

This book is for every level of sock knitter: from the timid beginner to the expert. However, if you've *never* knit a pair of socks before, I strongly recommend picking up a copy of *The Sock Project* or heading over to YouTube for some free tutorials. Knit a few pairs of basic socks and you'll be ready to tackle all the patterns in this book. Each design is labeled by difficulty level (Beginner, Advanced Beginner, and Intermediate), and all the skills you'll need to know are listed as well, making it easy for you to pick and choose what you want to knit according to your skill level.

If you aren't already obsessed with knitting socks, I can almost guarantee you will be by the time you've knit some of the patterns in this book. It's hard to resist the sock siren song once you've been encouraged to surround yourself with color and experiment with all you can do on these small, seemingly inconsequential little knits.

BEFORE WE BEGIN

Materials and Tools

Yarn Selection

Knitting is a bit of a trap. There's a common fallacy that if you make something yourself, it should be cheaper than if you bought it. I shared earlier that I mistakenly thought I could save money by knitting my own hats and sweaters and socks. The first time I walked into a yarn shop with a budget of thirty dollars, I thought I'd be able to buy enough yarn with that big wad of cash for at least two sweaters and a couple of hats. I *know*. So naive! I was floored when I saw that one skein—one!—would take my entire budget. Before tax.

Many new knitters suffer severe sticker shock when they see just how expensive wool can get. Fortunately, there are affordable options out there in the way of acrylic and acrylic/wool blends, but when you are knitting something for your feet, acrylic is probably the worst choice you can make. It's not breathable, meaning heat and sweat sort of . . . percolate under the fabric. That *ewww* face you just made? Indeed.

So, what *are* some good yarn choices for sock knitting? **Merino/nylon** blends are the gold standard, and the sock yarn you'll see the most. Typically coming in ratios of 75 percent merino/25 percent nylon (the most durable), to 80/20, to 90/10 (the least durable), these blends are an excellent choice because merino is a soft, warm, breathable wool, and the addition of nylon adds some strength to the fiber, since socks see so much friction from wear.

Additionally, you'll see some sock yarn that is made from **BFL/nylon** blends. The Bluefaced Leicester sheep is a hardy little fellow whose wool is a bit sturdier than merino. In general, the softer the wool, the more likely it is to wear and pill over time. The scratchier and tougher the wool, the more resistant it is to friction. Because people tend to like soft socks, not scratchy socks, merino is the breed of choice for most sock yarn manufacturers. The fabric you get from BFL blends is not quite as soft, but it's hardly like wearing a Brillo pad.

It's best to understand from the beginning that your socks *will* wear out. Wool is a natural fiber, and like all natural things, it's meant to break down and wear out eventually. Knit socks are a treasure, but they require a little maintenance in the form of darning and mending and general babying. Commercially produced socks will last longer, but you don't get to enjoy making them yourself and customizing them to your feet and unique personality.

Hand-knit socks are infinitely more satisfying to wear than plain old athletic socks, in my opinion. So let's dive into curating a stash that allows you to knit any kind of sock you want, at any time.

How to build a useful sock yarn stash

If you've followed me on social media or read my first book, you'll know I LOVE using color in my hand-knit socks. My wardrobe, however, is surprisingly muted. My mom walked into my closet once and couldn't tell which side was mine and which was my husband's. It was just a sea of grays, denim, black, and flannel.

But my socks? I go absolutely WILD with my socks. My favorite part of the design process is digging through my stash and looking for color combinations that make my heart sing. I call my supply closet my own personal local yarn store, because it's got pretty much everything I need to knit any kind of sock I could possibly want to knit. It took me years to collect, but I can show you how to get started curating your own personal sock yarn store, no matter your budget.

First, let's start with **tonals and solids**, which are what I use most.

Whether you want to knit stripes or colorwork, or let an intricate cable or texture pattern shine, tonals and solids are your best friends. A tonal yarn is typically dyed by hand, so you'll see some natural variation in how deep the color is saturated on the yarn. Solid yarn is typically commercially produced, so it's the same even shade all over.

I personally love the Knit Picks Stroll line of solid yarn for its color range and affordability. Lang Jawoll and Filcolana Arwetta are also great budget-friendly options for building a solid-colors stash. You can find all three brands online of course, and if you live in Europe, you're probably lucky enough to find Arwetta and Jawoll at your local grocery store or something. (I once heard a rumor that Europeans can buy yarn at the gas station. I don't know if this is true, but I desperately want to live in a world where you can fill your tank and grab a hank of wool at the same time.)

Tonal yarn is typically hand-dyed. There isn't a huge difference to the naked eye between a tonal and a solid, but if you compare them side by side, you'll see that the subtle variations in color depth on a tonal skein give it a bit of life, an interior glow.

Hand-dyed yarn is necessarily more expensive than commercially manufactured yarn. It's a treat for me, so over the years I've slowly collected tonals in every color so I have a good stash built up. You rarely ever use an entire 3½-ounce (100 g) skein of hand-dyed yarn to knit a pair of socks. Using a little here for a heel and toe, and a little there for some stripes means the more expensive tonal yarn skeins can contribute to dozens of socks!

What about **speckled and variegated yarn**?

We see those gorgeous skeins all over social media, and many a knitter has been tempted into emptying their bank account to get their grubby hands on those hand-dyed marvels. Are they good for sock knitting?

Yes and no. Basic socks are the best use for speckled and variegated yarns, in my opinion. They allow the yarn to do what it does best: show off. Use a heavily speckled or variegated yarn on a cable or lace sock, however, and your brain will overheat as you try to figure out what you should be looking at.

It's like putting on a couture gown and throwing a fishing net over yourself. You can sort of see the net, and you can sort of see the gown peeking through, but both things are canceling each other out. Intricate stitches have a tendency to get lost under all that artful dying, and the yarn itself seems to be pleading for some simplicity so it can show you just how beautiful it is.

I keep a small, thoughtful collection of speckles and variegated yarn in my stash. As you'll see in the patterns, there's definitely a time and place to bust them out, but for my money, investing in an expansive collection of solids and tonals serves me well in terms of the variety of socks one can knit.

Needles

There are many methods for knitting socks: magic loop, using double-pointed needles, using small circular needles, and using two long circular needles, just to name a few. Whatever method you prefer (fear not—there is no one "best" way), you'll need a small collection of needle sizes to ensure you are ready to knit any sock, anytime. Here's what I've got in my stash.

US size 1 (2.25 mm): for almost any kind of sock.

US size 2 (2.75 mm): for colorwork socks and cabled socks. Both reduce the stretch of your fabric, so bigger needles are handy for increasing the amount of fabric your sock has, which will help you haul it over your big heel.

US size 3 (3.25 mm): for thicker, DK-weight yarn socks.

OPPOSITE:
Since I prefer knitting magic loop, my favorite needles to use for sock knitting are long circulars.

I knit magic loop, so if that's your method as well, you'll want to ensure you are using circular needles at least 36" (91 cm) long. I like the ChiaoGoo 40"-long (102 cm) lace needles with the red cable.

For colorwork, I like to use small circular needles (pictured below) because I find they allow me to work faster and more efficiently, without much fuss. I like the ChiaoGoo TWIST Shorties because one needle is longer than the other, which, in my experience, reduces hand cramping.

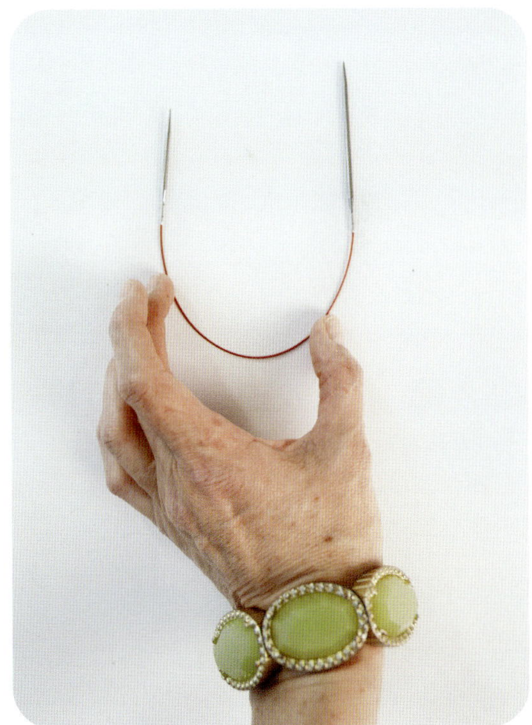

Notions

You'll need ring stitch markers. I use size 5 mm (which fit up to a US size 8 needle) and buy them in a multicolor set. I also like to keep bulb stitch markers handy for counting rounds, but these aren't strictly necessary. A good pair of snips, a measuring tape, and a tapestry needle for weaving in ends are a must for your basket or bag. Finally, a small cable needle (I like the green one that comes in the Clover brand variety pack) and a row counter will round out your kit. With these few tools, you'll be equipped to knit anything.

Sock Blockers

I hardly ever give directives when it comes to sock knitting. How you knit them, what colors you choose, what heels you like best—all of these matters are extremely personal and best left to the knitter. But on this one point I will make my opinion heard loud and clear: Please, PLEASE, please block your socks! You'll be so happy you did! Once it comes off the needles, especially if you've done colorwork, cables, or lace, your sock will look like it was pulled from the wreckage of a wooden ship that crashed in the Arctic 150 years ago. It will be lumpy, misshapen, exhausted, and thoroughly wrung out. Your stitches will be uneven. They'll seem slightly uncomfortable to be standing so close together. The fabric will be a little coarse from all that handling.

To revive your weary little sock, all you have to do is soak it in a little tub of lukewarm water and a dollop of wool wash. Let it luxuriate in the bubbles for a good twenty minutes, then gently squish the excess water out, wrap it in a towel, then stomp on it to get even more water out.

Next, you can place it on a sock blocker (my recommendation) or lay it out flat to dry on your bed. I like to turn on a fan to help it dry faster. My preferred sock blocker is the blue plastic kind from Knitter's Pride. They come in multiple sizes, and I've had mine for going on five years. They're very durable, as plastic things often are.

Once your little sock is dry, it will be transformed. No longer lumpy and misshapen, your sock will be smooth, slinky, squishy, and extra soft. Your stitches will be snuggled up to one another, their little legs even and straight. No lumps. No bumps. Just a delightfully smooth sock that drips through your hands like silk.

OPPOSITE:
Clockwise from top left: 1. Stitch markers, 2. tapestry needle, 3. cable needle, 4. row counter, 5. measuring tape, 6. snips, 7. project bag

ABOVE:
Sock blocker in action

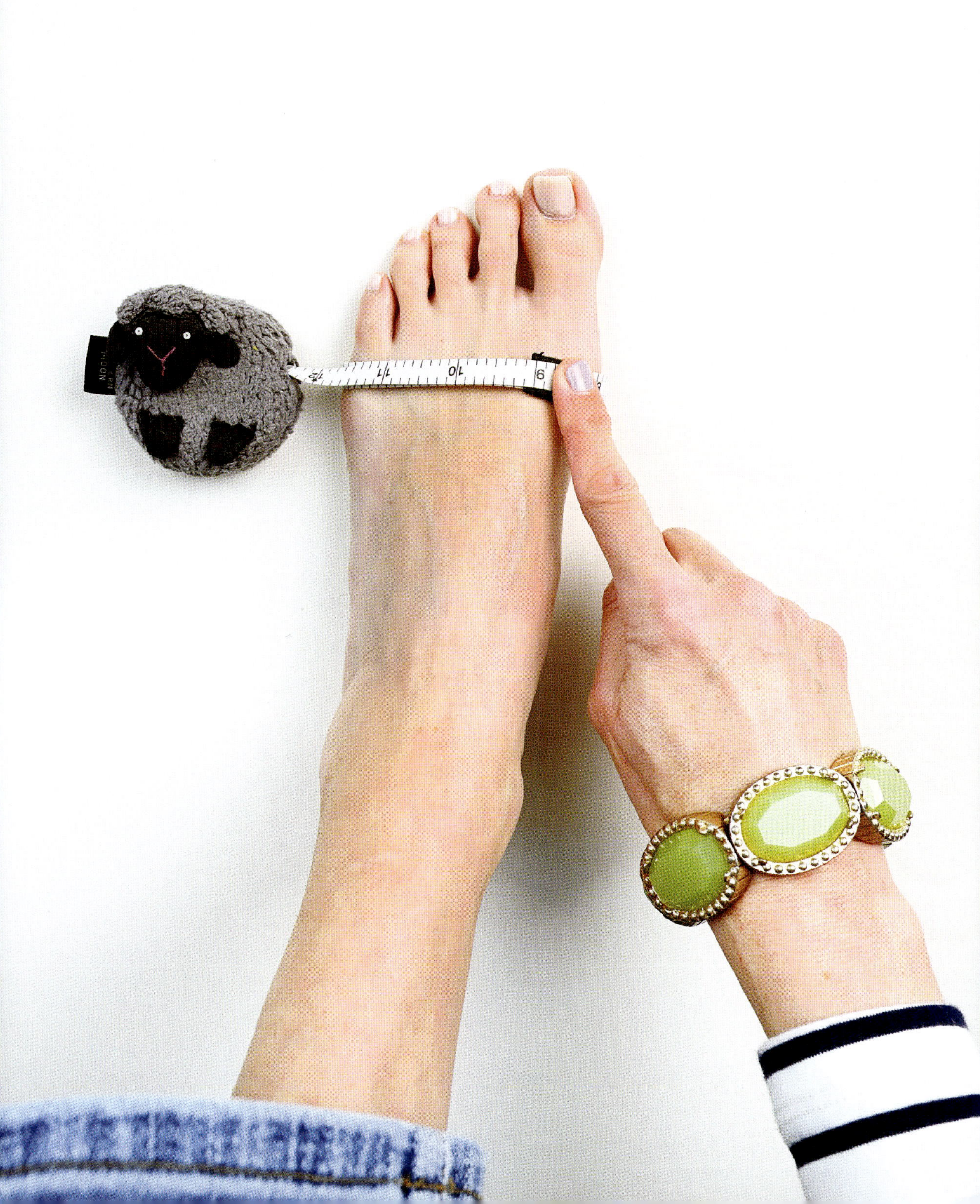

Tips and Tricks

Before we dive into the patterns, I think it's helpful to have a little library of tips and tricks you can incorporate as you work your way through the book. If you are a newer sock knitter, I advise reading through this chapter so you know what's included. If you come to a pattern that uses skills you haven't encountered, these tips and tricks should allow you to work through it. You'll find other tips scattered throughout the book as a particular pattern calls for them.

Sizing

My sizing is based on the circumference of the ball of your foot. To determine which size you should knit, simply wrap a tape measure around the ball of your foot to get your measurement. Next, choose the corresponding size that pairs with that measurement. The ball of my foot measures 8" (20 cm), so I always knit the size medium.

Some of you might measure *between* sizes. You might be wondering, What am I supposed to do if I measure 7½" (19 cm)? In that case, your personal knitting tension will give you a clue. Are you a tight knitter, meaning you typically get 9–10 stitches to a horizontal inch (2.5 cm) of knitting on US size 1 (2.25 mm) needles with fingering weight yarn? Knit the larger size! If you are a looser knitter, getting 7–8 stitches per horizontal inch (2.5 cm) of knitting, size down and knit the smaller size.

Knitting Colorwork

Knitting stranded colorwork on socks can be a little tricky. Socks must have an appropriate amount of stretch to fit over your heel. Floats, those little bars of yarn on the back of your fabric when you do stranded knitting, reduce the stretch of your sock.

To compensate for this, we've got to make more fabric. We can either add more stitches or use bigger needles. I personally like to use bigger needles, keeping my stitch counts the same, so almost all of the colorwork patterns in this book will direct you to go up a needle size.

However, some colorwork patterns require different stitch counts to make the motif, so you might be working with a larger stitch count and a smaller needle. It's always important to read through the pattern first so you have a clear picture of what chart to use, which size to knit, and which needles to employ.

In addition to making our fabric bigger, there are other ways we can ensure our fabric is stretchy enough to fit over our heels.

Keep your tension relaxed

As you work, keep your tension nice and loose. You don't want to yank hard on your contrast colors as you put the old yarn down and pick the new yarn up. Your floats should be relaxed on the back of your fabric, not pulled taut! I've found it's best not to knit colorwork socks if I'm angry, stressed, or watching a scary movie. You want to be as relaxed as possible so your floats stay drapey and loose.

The bars on the wrong side of colorwork fabric are called "floats."

Keep the stitches on your right-hand needle spread out

Don't let the stitches on your right-hand needle get bunched up.

They should be spread out as you work, that way your contrasting yarn has further to travel when you pick it up.

If your yarn is bunched, your contrast-color float will be shorter, which will cause your fabric to pucker. Puckered fabric almost always means your sock will be too tight!

The stitches on the right-hand needle are bunched up, which will pucker my fabric.

The stitches on the right-hand needle are spread out, which helps keep my floats loose, instead of tight.

Manage long floats

The old adage is that a float should be no longer than an inch. In sock knitting, theoretically, you could get away with a float that lasts 8–9 stitches. I do it all the time without any trouble. Some knitters worry about catching their toes on long floats; however, I've never found this to be a problem.

If you have a float that will be longer than 8 or 9 stitches, I recommend catching your float on the back of your work. Make sure not to catch it in the same place round after round, however, or it will show up as a line on the right side of your work. If you need to work a long float in the same place over several rounds, mix up where you catch it. Maybe on stitch 4 of the repeat on the first round, and then stitch 6 on the next, and then the fifth stitch on the third, and so on.

Knit the next stitch as normal.

Flick the yarn you aren't using over the left needle.

Your float was caught on the wrong side of your work!

Knitting Stripes

Stripes can seem daunting to knitters who don't want to weave in all those ends. Luckily, there's an easy trick for knitting in ends as you go.

When you have 9 stitches left in the round, lay your new yarn strand over your working yarn strand. Knit the next stitch as normal.

Flick the new yarn over your left needle and knit the next stitch. Then knit another stitch as normal. Repeat these two steps, flicking the new yarn over the needle every other stitch until you reach the end of the round. Once you finish knitting in your new color, repeat these same steps over the first 8 stitches of your new round, this time knitting in your old color.

When you finish your sock, turn it wrong side out. You'll see a hairy little mess in there.

Give all those ends a gentle tug.

Then snip them down to about ½" (1 cm) long.

And that's it!

Additionally, you get a jog while knitting stripes when you change from one color to the next. Since you are knitting a spiral, not a perfect circle, your stitches don't line up evenly when you switch colors. There's an easy fix for that too.

On the first stitch of the second round of your new color, lift up the right leg of the stitch below (which will be in your old color), and place it on the left-hand needle.

Then knit that leg together with the first stitch on the needle. And that's it! Continue knitting as normal in your new color.

Do you want to knit a striped cuff without the unsightly purl bumps you get from changing colors?

If you look closely,
you can see the purl bumps when I changed colors.

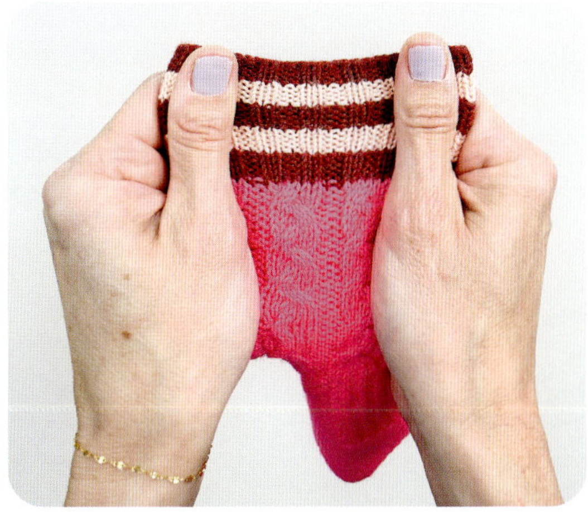

(On this sock, no purl bumps!)

There's a simple solution for that: When you change colors, knit that first round in the new color as Stockinette, then go back to your ribbing pattern for the remainder of that color. When you switch colors again, repeat. Knit the first round even in Stockinette, then go back to the ribbing for the subsequent rounds. No purl bumps!

Chapter 1

TRADITIONAL SOCKS

What better way to kick off this book than by diving into knitting traditions from around the world? Certain motifs, cable patterns, and textural stitches are classics. They are the foundational language we use to practice this ancient and beloved craft.

Oversized Aran sweaters from Ireland, sampler garments from the Channel Islands, cheerful two-color stranded motifs from Norway, and graphic floral patterns inspired by the famed knitted mittens of Latvia all inspired the socks in this chapter. The lovely thing about drawing inspiration from the timeless stitches of the past is translating the old into something new and decidedly personal to *you*.

Color, as always, is the start of my process when building a knitted garment stitch by stitch. Whether you add your own style into these patterns with tonal yarns, new color combinations, or a wild foray into neon or speckled yarns, I hope you enjoy knitting these timeless designs as much as I did.

Latvian Rose Socks

Tulips are always a favorite!

Every week I buy fresh flowers for my house at the grocery store. Tulips are a favorite, as are ranunculus and peonies. I don't make fancy bouquets or elaborate arrangements. I simply plop them in a vase and admire their simple charm. Florals are not a groundbreaking motif for colorwork knitting, but they're a favorite for a reason. They look so graphic and eye-catching on a pair of socks.

The famed mittens of Latvia, with their eclectic color combinations and striking patterns, were the inspiration for these sweet floral socks. I created a moody spring vibe with the dark green background, but the beauty of this pattern is how well it can translate seasonally simply by choosing a different color palette.

DIFFICULTY LEVEL

Advanced beginner

SKILLS

Stranded knitting
Afterthought heel

MATERIALS

Yarn

La Bien Aimée Super Sock [75% superwash merino/25% nylon; 465 yards (425 m); 3½ ounces (100 g)]: (102) 121 (144, 168, 189) yards [(93) 111 (132, 154, 173) m] in Emeline (MC)

Coates & Co. Cottage Sock [75% superwash merino/25% nylon; 437 yards (400 m); 3½ ounces (100 g)]: (28) 36 (42, 51, 68) yards [(26) 33 (38, 47, 62) m] in Color No. 08 Bright Peach (CC1)

Cascade Heritage [75% superwash merino/25% nylon; 437 yards (400 m); 3½ ounces (100 g)]: (28) 36 (42, 51, 68) yards [(26) 33 (38, 47, 62) m] in 5612 Moss (CC2)

Needles

US size 1 (2.25 mm)
US size 2 (2.75 mm)

Notions

Measuring tape, stitch markers (including a clasp marker), snips, tapestry needle

GAUGE

36 sts = 4" (10 cm), knit in colorwork pattern in the round on US size 2 (2.75 mm) needles and blocked

SIZES

(Kid) S (M, L, XL)

MEASUREMENTS

The numbers below refer to the circumference of the ball of the foot, not the measurements of the finished sock.

(5–6) 7 (8, 9, 10)" [(13–15) 18 (20, 23, 25) cm]

LATVIAN ROSE CHART

You can work the chart in two different orientations. If you prefer your roses to cascade *down* the sock (as I did in the sample pair), knit Chart A. If you prefer your roses to cascade *up* the sock, knit Chart B.

Chart A

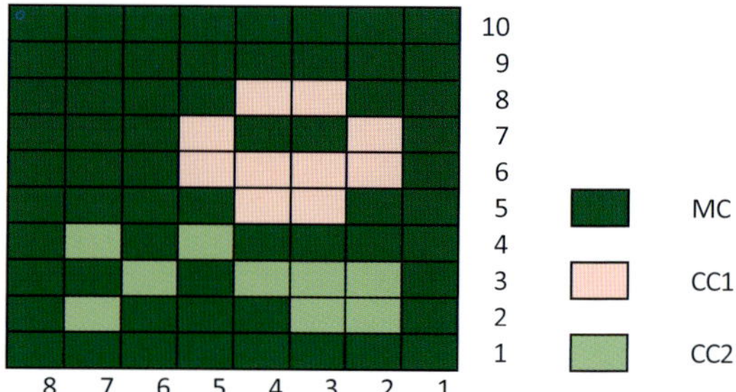

Chart B

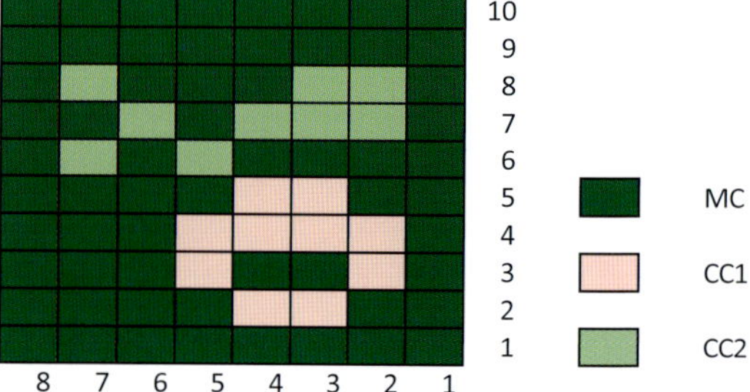

INSTRUCTIONS

Cuff

With US size 1 (2.25 mm) needles and MC, CO **(48) 57 (63, 72, 81)** sts and join for working in the rnd, being careful not to twist your sts. Est 2×1 ribbing: [k2, p1] to end.

Cont working the ribbing until your Cuff measures ¾" (2 cm), or your desired length.

Leg

Switch to US size 2 (2.75 mm) needles and work 1 rnd even in Stockinette, making the following inc or dec according to your size:

Kid: No inc or dec. **48 sts.**
S: Work to last 3 sts, k2tog, k1. **56 sts.**
M: Work to last 2 sts, kfb, k1. **64 sts.**
L: No inc or dec. **72 sts.**
XL: Work to last 3 sts, k2tog, k1. **80 sts.**

Begin working Latvian Rose Chart. Repeat all 10 rnds of the chart until the Leg (including Cuff) measures 4½" (11 cm), or your desired length. In my sample pair, I knit 3 roses before stopping to mark the Heel. Make sure to end *after* working rnd 9 of the chart!

Placing the Marker for the Afterthought Heel

Once you've decided your Leg is long enough, on the next rnd (you should be on rnd 10 of the chart), simply knit **(36) 42 (48, 54, 60)** sts and clip a clasp marker onto that last st you just knit. Then just keep knitting to the end of the rnd. You have now marked where your Afterthought Heel will eventually go, and you should now be ready to work rnd 1 of the chart.

Foot

Cont repeating all 10 rnds of the chart until your Foot reaches the desired length. The Craft Yarn Council has issued the following guidelines for the Foot of a sock, measured from the back of the Heel to the end of the Toe. (All sizes are US.)

Kid: 6–7½" (15–19 cm)
Women's shoe sizes 4–6.5: 8–9" (20.25–23 cm)
Women's shoe sizes 7–9.5: 9¼–10" (23.5–25.5 cm)
Women's shoe sizes 10–12.5: 10¼–11" (26–28 cm)
Men's shoe sizes 6–8.5: 9¼–10" (23.5–25.5 cm)
Men's shoe sizes 9–11.5: 10¼–11" (26–28 cm)
Men's shoe sizes 12–14: 11¼–12" (28.5–30.5 cm)

When working an Afterthought Heel, you need to take into account both your Heel length and your Toe length (they will be the same).

Kid: 1¼" (3 cm)
S: 1½" (4 cm)
M: 1½" (4 cm)
L: 1½" (4 cm)
XL: 1¾" (4 cm)

Now, take your desired Foot length, from the back of the Heel to end of the Toe, and subtract both your Heel and Toe measurements. For example, my desired Foot length is 9" (23 cm). I subtract my Toe (1½" [4 cm]) and my Heel (1½" [4 cm]) and that leaves me with 6" (15 cm) I need to knit before starting my Toe decreases.

Toe

Break CC colors and switch back to US size 1 (2.25 mm) needles. Using MC, knit 1 rnd even in Stockinette, then decrease to shape your Toe:

Rnd 1: K1, ssk, k**(18) 22 (26, 30, 34)** sts, k2tog, k1, pm, k1, ssk, k**(18) 22 (26, 30, 34)** sts, k2tog, k1.

Rnd 2: Knit.

Rnd 3: K1, ssk, knit to 3 sts before next marker, k2tog, k1, sl m, k1, ssk, knit around to 3 sts before end of rnd, k2tog, k1.

Repeat rnds 2 and 3 until **(20) 24 (28, 32, 36)** sts remain. Use Kitchener Stitch to close up your Toe.

Knitting the Afterthought Heel

You should have a long tube with a Cuff at one end and a Toe at the other. Go to the point in your tube where you placed the clasp marker. Make sure your tube is pressed flat. Half your sts should be facing up at you and the other half facing down. Your Toe should look like a wedge, with decrease lines on the sides of the wedge.

Identify the line of sts directly below the clasp marker. Select the first st at the edge of your tube. With US size 1 (2.25 mm) needles, insert the needle into the right leg of that first st. Next, insert the needle into the right leg of the second st, and then into the right leg of the third st. Cont inserting your needle into the right leg of every st until you have picked up **(24) 28 (32, 36, 40)** sts. Next, repeat that process for the line of sts on the other side of your marked st. You should have **(48) 56 (64, 72, 80)** sts total divided evenly on your needles.

Remove the marker and tease that st up with your tapestry needle. Snip that st, being very careful not to snip anything else! Use your tapestry needle to tease out the yarn you've snipped from the sts. Start in the middle and go to the end on either side of your snipped st.

You now have a gaping hole in your sock tube and live Heel sts on the needles, ready to be worked. You also have a strand of yarn dangling on each side of the hole. Those will come in handy later when you weave in your ends. I use them to close gaps at the corners of the Heel.

You will work your Afterthought Heel the same as your Toe. Join in your yarn. Sizes **Kid** and **L**, work 3 rnds even in Stockinette, then move on to the Heel Decreases below. Sizes **S, M, XL** ONLY, work the following setup rnd prior to working the Heel:

S: K1, ssk, k25, k2tog, knit around to end. **52 sts.**
M: K1, ssk, k31, k2tog, knit around to end. **64 sts.**
XL: K1, ssk, k37, k2tog, knit around to end. **76 sts.**

Work 2 more rnds even in Stockinette, then begin working the Heel Decreases.

Rnd 1: K1, ssk, k **(18) 22 (26, 30, 34)** sts, k2tog, k1, pm, k1, ssk, k **(18) 22 (26, 30, 34)** sts, k2tog, k1.

Rnd 2: Knit.

Rnd 3: K1, ssk, knit to 3 sts before next marker, k2tog, k1, sl m, k1, ssk, knit around to 3 sts before end of rnd, k2tog, k1.

Repeat rnds 2 and 3 until **(20) 24 (28, 32, 36)** sts remain.

Note: You can adjust the depth and fit of your Heel by working more or fewer decrease rnds. Try the sock on occasionally as you work your decreases to see how it's fitting. Stop your decreases when you can easily pinch the fabric closed.

Use Kitchener Stitch to close up your Heel.

Finishing

Weave in all your ends and block your socks.

Aran Sweater Socks

Do you ever feel like the world, and more broadly the entire universe, is nothing less than a swirling vector of chaos, and it is absolute madness to even step foot out your front door when gravity could stop working, or the moon could careen off into space, or General Mills could suddenly decide to discontinue Cinnamon Toast Crunch? Most days I feel like very little is under my direct locus of control. What do I do to quell the crushing anxiety of living in a wondrous but inherently dangerous world?

I walk. And I walk and I walk and I walk. Every morning and every evening, dragging my reluctant mutt Beesly along with me. We get sunlight on our little faces, and we observe the mallards paddling gently around the ponds. (They seem unbothered by the fact that if it weren't for the vacuum of space, we would be able to *hear* the sun, and apparently it sounds like a jackhammer. Terrifying.)

When one is walking relentlessly, day in and day out, rain or shine, through even the bitterest winter days, one needs a sturdy sweater. I didn't have time to knit my own (because socks), so I ordered a traditional cabled Aran sweater all the way from Ireland.

Three years later, it still looks new and is the coziest sweater I own. Naturally, I wanted that same cozy factor for my feet as well, so having a good cabled sock pattern in this book was a must.

My beloved Irish Aran sweater

These socks feature braided cables, which look quite intricate but are still easy to knit. Knit them in bold colors with a snappy striped cuff as I did, or hearken back to traditional Aran knitting with classic oatmeal, navy blue, or rich forest green. Either way, as you hike along on your own local walking path, think of me strolling on mine, each of us lost in our thoughts.

DIFFICULTY LEVEL

Advanced beginner

SKILLS

Cable knitting

Heel flap and gusset

MATERIALS

Yarn

Coates & Co. Cottage Sock [75% superwash merino wool/25% nylon; 437 yards (400 m); 3½ ounces (100 g)]: 178 (208, 246, 279) yards [163 (190, 225, 255) m] in Color No. 27 Fuchsia (MC)

Knit Picks Stroll [75% fine superwash merino/25% nylon; 231 yards (211 m); 1¾ ounces (50 g)]: 16 (21, 27, 32) yards [15 (19, 25, 29) m] in Cranberry Heather (CC1)

Coates & Co. Cottage Sock: 10 (16, 21, 26) yards [9 (15, 19, 24) m] in Color No. 07 Light Peach (CC2)

Needles

US size 1 (2.25 mm)

US size 2 (2.75 mm)

Notions

Measuring tape, stitch markers, snips, tapestry needle

GAUGE

38 sts = 4" (10 cm), knit in Braided Cable Pattern on US size 2 (2.75mm) needles in the round and blocked

SIZES

S (M, L, XL)

MEASUREMENTS

The numbers below refer to the circumference of the ball of the foot, not the measurements of the finished sock.

7 (8, 9, 10)" [18 (20, 23, 25) cm]

BRAIDED CABLE CHART

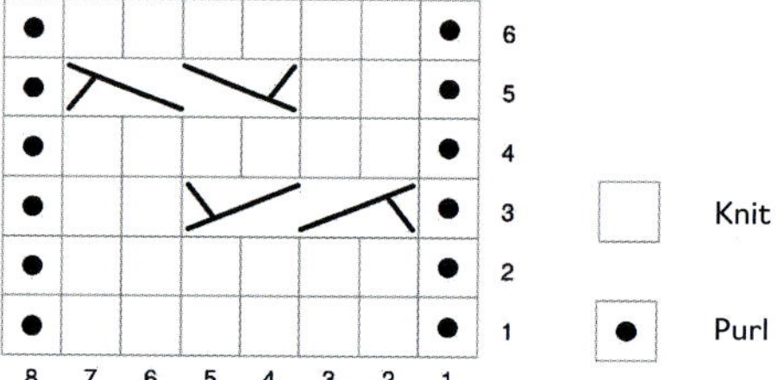

Slip 2 stitches to cable needle and hold in back; k2, k2 from cable needle

Slip 2 stitches to cable needle and hold in front; k2, k2 from cable needle

BRAIDED CABLE WRITTEN INSTRUCTIONS

C4B (Cable 4 Back): Slip 2 sts to cable needle and hold in back. K2, k2 from cable needle.

C4F (Cable 4 Front): Slip 2 sts to cable needle and hold in front. K2, k2 from cable needle.

Rnds 1, 2, 4, and 6: P1, k6 [p2, k6] **5 (6, 7, 8)** times, p2, k6, p1.

Rnd 3: P1, C4B, k2 [p2, C4B, k2] **5 (6, 7, 8)** times, p2, C4B, k2, p1.

Rnd 5: P1, k2, C4F [p2, k2, C4F] **5 (6, 7, 8)** times, p2, k2, C4F, p1.

INSTRUCTIONS

Cuff

With CC1 and US size 1 (2.25 mm) needles, CO **56 (64, 72, 80)** sts and join for working in the rnd. Est 2×2 ribbing: [k2, p2] to end.

Work 4 more rnds of ribbing in CC1, then join in CC2 and work 5 rnds of ribbing. Work 5 rnds in CC1, then 5 rnds in CC2, then finish with 5 rnds of CC1. Your Cuff should measure approximately 2" (5 cm).

Tip: To create neat striped ribbing without purl bumps, simply knit the first round of each stripe in Stockinette. For example, when switching from the cranberry stripe to the light peach stripe, I knit the first round of light peach in Stockinette, then worked the remaining four rounds of the light peach in the k2, p2 ribbing. When I switched back to the cranberry yarn, I repeated this process. No purl bumps! ☺

Leg

Cut CC color and switch to US size 2 (2.75 mm) needles. Since cables reduce the stretch of our knitted fabric, we need to work them on bigger needles so our socks won't choke our legs in a death grip!

Join in MC and begin working Braided Cable Pattern. Repeat all 6 rnds of the pattern until your Leg (including Cuff) measures 5½" (14 cm), or your desired length. Stop for the Heel *after* completing rnd 1.

Heel Flap

Work in Braided Cable Pattern (you should be on rnd 2) across the first **28 (32, 36, 40)** sts, then begin working your Heel Flap back and forth across the remaining **28 (32, 36, 40)** sts as follows:

Row 1 (RS): K2, [slip 1, k1] to end. Turn work.

Row 2 (WS): Slip 1 wyif, purl to end. Turn work.

Row 3: [Slip 1, k1] to end. Turn work.

Repeat rows 2 and 3 until Heel Flap measures **2 (2, 2¼, 2½)" [5 (5, 6, 6.5) cm]**. End *after* you have worked row 3.

Heel Turn

Row 1 (WS): Slip 1 wyif, p**14 (16, 18, 20)**, p2tog, p1, turn.

Row 2 (RS): Slip 1, k3, ssk, k1, turn.

Row 3: Slip 1 wyif, p4, p2tog, p1, turn.

Row 4: Slip 1, k5, ssk, k1, turn.

You have now established the following pattern for your Heel Turn: Slip 1, knit or purl to 1 st before the gap created by turning on the previous row, ssk or p2tog, k1 or p1, turn. Cont in this pattern until all your Heel sts have been worked, ending on a RS row. You should now have **16 (18, 20, 22)** Heel sts.

Gusset

With the right side of your work facing, pick up and knit **12 (14, 16, 18)** sts along the left side of your Heel Flap.

Next, work in Braided Cable Pattern across the **28 (32, 36, 40)** sts that we've left undisturbed on our needles while working our Heel Flap. Pm, and pick up **12 (14, 16, 18)** sts on the right side of the Heel Flap. Knit across the Heel sts, then knit down the first set of new sts you picked up on the left side. You've reached the end of the rnd, and all your sts have now been picked up. You should now have **68 (78, 88, 98)** sts on your needles.

Gusset Decreases

Rnd 1: Work in Braided Cable Pattern across **28 (32, 36, 40)** sts, sl m, k1, ssk, knit around to 3 sts before the end of rnd, k2tog, k1.

Rnd 2: Work even with no decreases.

Repeat these two rnds until you have **56 (64, 72, 80)** sts on your needles.

Foot

Cont working in Braided Cable Pattern across the first **28 (32, 36, 40)** sts, and working Stockinette (knit every st) across the remaining **28 (32, 36, 40)** sts until your Foot reaches just to the tip of your pinky toe. End *after* working rnd 6 or rnd 1. If you can't easily try on your socks as you knit (working on double-pointed needles or tiny circulars can make this challenging), or if you are knitting gift socks for some lucky recipient, the Craft Yarn Council has issued the following length guidelines for the Foot of a sock, measured from the back of the Heel to the end of the Toe.

(All sizes are US.)

Women's shoe sizes 4–6.5: 8–9" (20.25–23 cm)
Women's shoe sizes 7–9.5: 9¼–10" (23.5–25.5 cm)
Women's shoe sizes 10–12.5: 10¼–11" (26–28 cm)
Men's shoe sizes 6–8.5: 9¼–10" (23.5–25.5 cm)
Men's shoe sizes 9–11.5: 10¼–11" (26–28 cm)
Men's shoe sizes 12–14: 11¼–12" (28.5–30.5 cm)

When working a Heel Flap and Gusset, you need to take into account your Toe length.

S: 1½" (4 cm)
L: 1½" (4 cm)
M: 1½" (4 cm)
XL: 1¾" (4 cm)

Now, take your desired Foot length, from the back of the Heel to the end of the Toe, and subtract your Toe measurement. For example, my desired Foot length is 9" (23 cm). I subtract my Toe (1½" [4 cm]) and that leaves me with 7½" (19 cm) I need to knit before starting my Toe decreases. Measure starting at the back of the Heel.

Toe

Rnd 1: K1, ssk, k**22 (26, 30, 34)** sts, k2tog, k1, pm, k1, ssk, k**22 (26, 30, 34)** sts, k2tog, k1.

Rnd 2: Knit.

Rnd 3: K1, ssk, knit to 3 sts before next marker, k2tog, k1, sl m, k1, ssk, knit around to 3 sts before end of rnd, k2tog, k1.

Repeat rnds 2 and 3 until **24 (28, 32, 36)** sts remain.

Use Kitchener Stitch to close up your Toe.

Finishing

Weave in all your ends and block your socks.

Blomst Socks

When I was a kid growing up in the dry, snowless plains of rural Oklahoma, I was obsessed with this illustrated book about gnomes. We had a copy in the school library, and I would tuck myself into a corner with that big book spread open on my lap, making myself sick with longing. Oh, to be a gnome living in the far north, dodging the footfalls of reindeer and gathering firewood in the snow for my little gnome home.

Norwegian stranded sweaters, with their colorful motifs of snowflakes, flowers, and reindeer, evoke the same feeling I got as a child lost in that magical gnome book. They are good cheer made manifest in a tangible artifact that keeps you warm. I feel an interior glow when I slip a Norwegian sweater over my head and bury myself in the warm luxury of good wool and tradition.

The Blomst Socks are what I imagine a Norwegian gnome would wear on her little feet. Following the chart, and watching the motif develop round by round and stitch by stitch, is a joy. Whether you choose a more modern neon color palette or stick to the primary colors of old, these socks will make you gnome-book-level happy every time you wear them!

The infamous Gnome book!

DIFFICULTY LEVEL

Intermediate

SKILLS

Stranded knitting
Managing long floats
Afterthought heel

MATERIALS

Yarn

Coates & Co. Cottage Sock [75% superwash merino wool/25% nylon; 437 yards (400 m); 3½ ounces (100 g)]: 42 (51, 68, 82) yards [38 (47, 62, 75) m] in Color No. 27 Fuchsia (MC)

Coates & Co. Cottage Sock: 33 (40, 52, 64) yards [30 (37, 48, 58) m] in Color No. 11 Electric Yellow (CC1)

Coates & Co. Cottage Sock: 14 (19, 25, 30) yards [13 (17, 23, 27) m] in Color No. 20 Dark Teal (CC2)

Coates & Co. Cottage Sock: 12 (17, 23, 28) yards [11 (16, 21, 27) m] in Color No. 43 Atmosphere (CC3)

Coates & Co. Cottage Sock: 26 (34, 42, 50) yards [24 (31, 38, 46) m] in Color No. 08 Bright Peach (CC4)

Needles

US size 1 (2.25 mm)
US size 2 (2.75 mm)

Notions

Measuring tape, stitch markers (including a clasp marker), snips, tapestry needle

GAUGE

32 sts = 4" (10 cm), knit in colorwork pattern in the round on US size 2 (2.75 mm) needles and blocked

SIZES

S (M, L, XL)

MEASUREMENTS

The numbers below refer to the circumference of the ball of the foot, not the measurements of the finished sock.

7 (8, 9, 10)" [18 (20, 23, 25) cm]

BLOMST BORDER CHART

Border Chart (All Sizes)

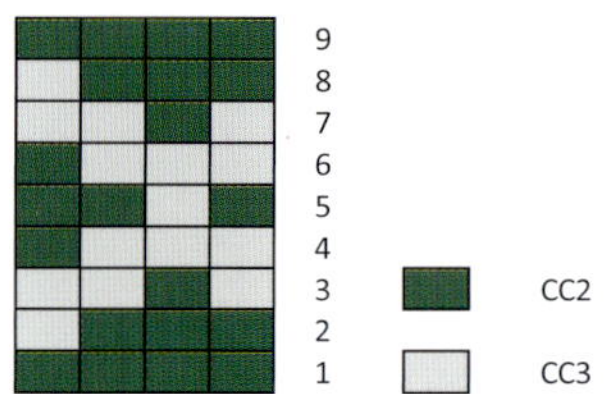

BLOMST FLORAL CHARTS

Floral Charts (SMALL, MEDIUM, LARGE, XL)

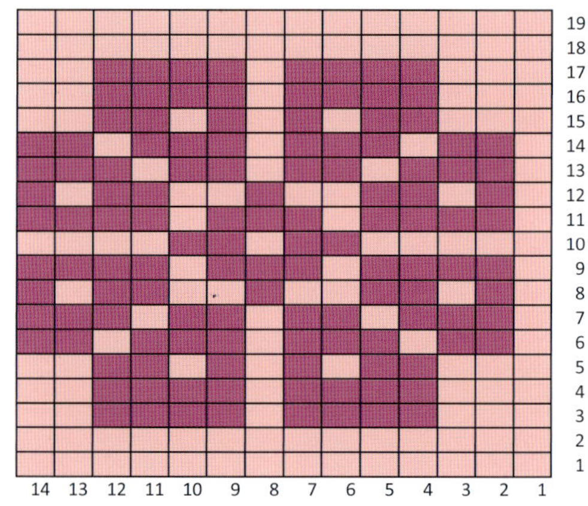

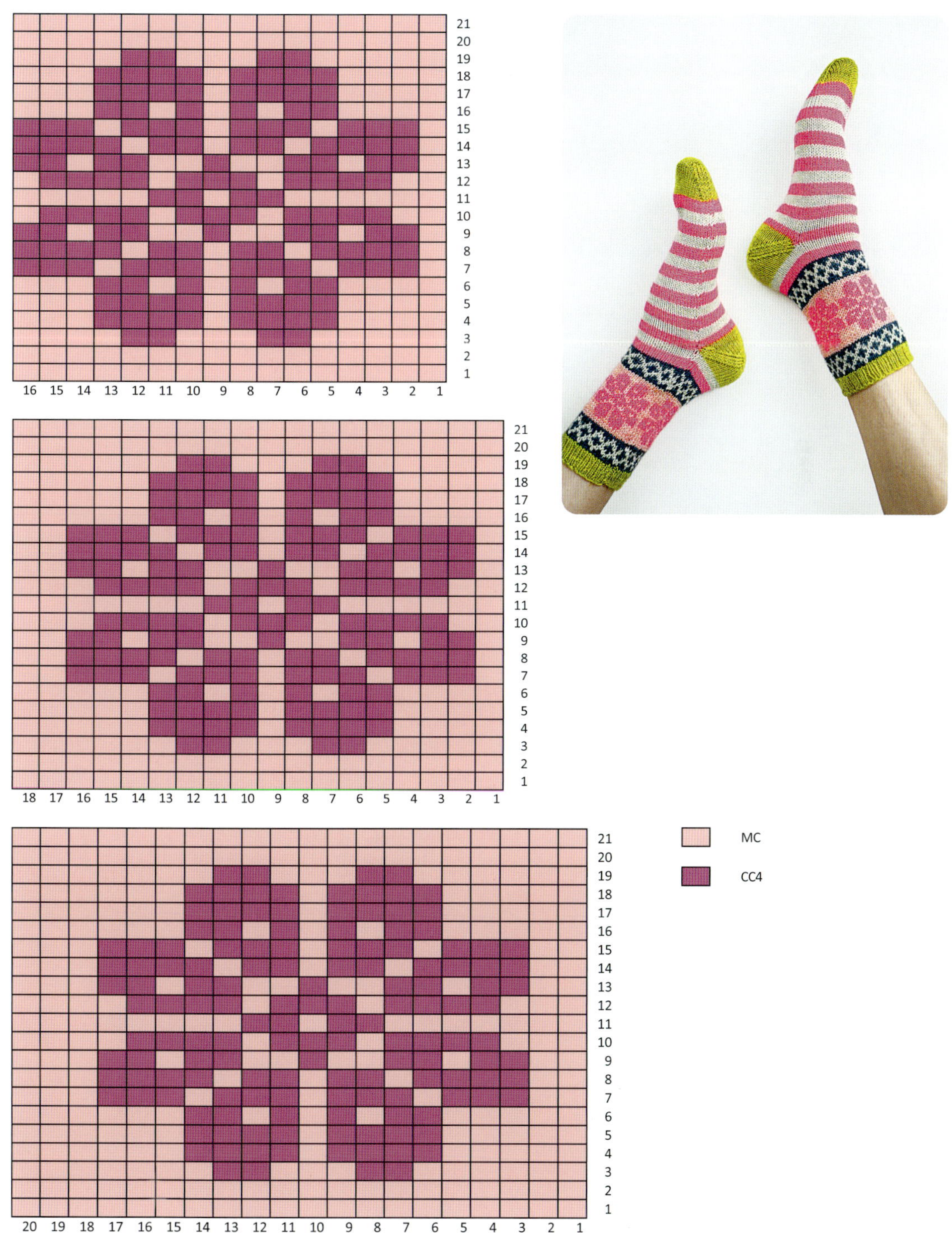
MC
CC4

INSTRUCTIONS

Cuff

With CC1 and US size 1 (2.25 mm) needles, CO **57 (63, 72, 81)** sts and join for working in the rnd, being careful not to twist your sts. Est 2×1 ribbing: [k2, p1] to end.

Cont working the ribbing until your Cuff measures ¾" (2 cm), or your desired length. On the last rnd of the ribbing, we need to get our stitch count back to an even number. If you are working the size **L**, you already have an even number and can move on to the Leg instructions. The rest of you, make the following increase or decrease according to your size:

S: Work in rib pattern to the last 3 sts, k2tog, p1. **56 sts.**

M: Work in rib pattern to the last 3 sts, kfb, k1, p1. **64 sts.**

XL: Work in rib pattern to the last 3 sts, k2tog, p1. **80 sts.**

Leg

Cut CC1 and switch to US size 2 (2.75 mm) needles. Work all 9 rnds of the Blomst Border Chart *once*. Next, work the Blomst Floral Chart that corresponds to your size *once*. Finally, work all 9 rnds of the Blomst Border Chart *once*.

Cut CC2 and join in MC. Switch back to US size 1 (2.25 mm) needles and with MC, work 5 rnds even in Stockinette (knit every rnd). Next, work 5 rnds even in CC3. You are now done with the Leg.

Note: You can work more 5-rnd stripes if you prefer your Leg to be longer. The Leg on my sample pair, knit as explained above, measures 5½" (14 cm).

Placing the Marker for the Afterthought Heel

With MC, knit **42 (48, 54, 60)** sts and clip a clasp marker onto that last st you just knit. Then just keep knitting to the end of the rnd. You have now marked where your Afterthought Heel will eventually go.

Foot

Work 4 more rnds in MC, then 5 rnds in CC3. Cont knitting 5-rnd stripes alternating between MC and CC3 until your Foot reaches your desired length. The Craft Yarn Council has issued the following guidelines for the Foot of a sock, measured from the back of the Heel to the end of the Toe.

(All sizes are US.)
Women's shoe sizes 4–6.5: 8–9" (20.25–23 cm)
Women's shoe sizes 7–9.5: 9¼–10" (23.5–25.5 cm)
Women's shoe sizes 10–12.5: 10¼–11" (26–28 cm)
Men's shoe sizes 6–8.5: 9¼–10" (23.5–25.5 cm)
Men's shoe sizes 9–11.5: 10¼–11" (26–28 cm)
Men's shoe sizes 12–14: 11¼–12" (28.5–30.5 cm)

When working an Afterthought Heel, you need to take into account both your Heel length and your Toe length (they will be the same).

S: 1½" (4 cm)
M: 1½" (4 cm)
L: 1½" (4 cm)
XL: 1¾" (4 cm)

Now, take your desired Foot length, from the back of the Heel to the end of the Toe, and subtract both your Heel and Toe measurements. For example, my desired Foot length is 9" (23 cm). I subtract my Toe (1½" [4 cm]) and my Heel (1½" [4 cm]) and that leaves me with 6" (15 cm) I need to knit before starting my toe decreases.

Toe

Break MC and CC3. Using CC1, knit 1 rnd even in Stockinette, then begin the following decrease pattern to shape your Toe:

Rnd 1: K1, ssk, k**22 (26, 30, 34)** sts, k2tog, k1, pm, k1, ssk, k**22 (26, 30, 34)** sts, k2tog, k1.

Rnd 2: Knit.

Rnd 3: K1, ssk, knit to 3 sts before next marker, k2tog, k1, sl m, k1, ssk, knit around to 3 sts before end of rnd, k2tog, k1.

Repeat rnds 2 and 3 until **24 (28, 32, 36)** sts remain.

Use Kitchener Stitch to close up your Toe.

Knitting the Afterthought Heel

You should have a long tube with a Cuff at one end and a Toe at the other end. Go to the point in your tube where you placed the clasp marker. Make sure your tube is pressed flat. You should have half your sts facing up at you and the other half of your sts facing down. Your Toe should look like a wedge, with the decrease lines on the sides of the wedge.

Identify the line of sts directly below the clasp marker. Select the first st at the edge of your tube. With US size 1 (2.25 mm) needles, insert the needle into the right leg of that first st.

Next, insert the needle into the right leg of the second st, and then into the right leg of the third st. Cont inserting your needle into the right leg of every st until you have picked up **28 (32, 36, 40)** sts. Next, repeat that process for the line of sts on the other side of your waste yarn. You should have **56 (64, 72, 80)** sts total on your needles ready to be knit.

Join in CC1 and knit 2 rnds even in Stockinette, then begin the following decrease pattern for your Heel:

Rnd 1: K1, ssk, k**22 (26, 30, 34)** sts, k2tog, k1, pm, k1, ssk, k**22 (26, 30, 34)** sts, k2tog, k1.

Rnd 2: Knit.

Rnd 3: K1, ssk, knit to 3 sts before next marker, k2tog, k1, sl m, k1, ssk, knit around to 3 sts before end of rnd, k2tog, k1.

Repeat rnds 2 and 3 until **24 (28, 32, 36)** sts remain.

Note: You can adjust the depth and fit of your Heel by working more or fewer decrease rnds. Try the sock on occasionally as you work your decreases to see how it's fitting. Stop your decreases when you can easily pinch the fabric closed.

Use Kitchener Stitch to close up your Heel.

Finishing

Weave in all your ends and block your socks.

Channel Island Socks

I love a good appetizer platter. Give me mini egg rolls, fried potato skins, quesadillas, and sliders, all in one meal. No need to stick to one culinary tradition! I want to visit the world when I go to a mid-tier family restaurant chain, grabbing at those bite-sized wonders like a crazed orangutan.

The same can be said for socks. Why limit yourself to one stitch pattern when you can try them all? Sampler socks are a brilliant way to not only display dazzling layers of texture, but to find out what you enjoy knitting and what stitches you'll happily forget. (For me that would be moss stitch. I love how it looks, but I'd rather swim in a murky, turtle-infested lake than knit it.)

The remote Channel Islands off the coast of Britain produced the infamous Guernsey (or gansey) sweaters, worn in old photos by haunted-looking fishermen. Featuring a delightful mix of stitch patterns, these sweaters are part of knitting lore, timeless garments that evoke a feeling of life persevering, even under brutal conditions.

The Channel Island Socks are soft and drapey, owing to the varied textures of the stitch patterns, but not to worry. That chunky ribbed cuff will keep them from falling down around your ankles. The resulting sock is soft, squishy, and subtly dramatic, especially knit in a lightly speckled yarn with a surprising pop of color at the toe.

We look super happy because we're on our way to stuff our faces with appetizers.

DIFFICULTY LEVEL

Advanced beginner

SKILLS

Yarn overs

Decrease stitches

Heel flap and gusset

MATERIALS

Yarn

Little Lionhead Knits Fingering Weight Soft Sock [85% superwash merino/15% nylon; 437 yards (400 m); 3½ ounces (100 g)]: 146 (172, 204, 238) yards [134 (157, 187, 218) m] in Carousel of Time (MC)

Hedgehog Fibres Sock [90% superwash merino/10% nylon; 437 yards (400 m); 3½ ounces (100 g)]: 14 (20, 24, 29) yards [13 (18, 22, 27) m] in Minty (CC)

Needles

US size 1 (2.25 mm)

Notions

Measuring tape, stitch markers, snips, tapestry needle

GAUGE

38 sts = 4" (10 cm), knit in 2×2 Rib Pattern in the round and blocked

38 sts = 4" (10 cm), knit in Double Moss Pattern in the round and blocked

32 sts = 4" (10 cm), knit in Lace Pennant Pattern in the round and blocked

SIZES

S (M, L, XL)

MEASUREMENTS

The numbers below refer to the circumference of the ball of the foot, not the measurements of the finished sock.

7 (8, 9, 10)" [18 (20, 23, 25) cm]

2×2 RIB PATTERN

Repeat the rnd 14 times.

Rnd 1: [K2, p2] to end.

GARTER RIDGE BORDER

Repeat all 4 rnds once.

Rnd 1: Purl.
Rnd 2: Knit.
Rnd 3: Purl.
Rnd 4: Knit.

DOUBLE MOSS PATTERN

Repeat all 4 rnds 3 times.

Rnds 1 and 2: [K2, p2] to end.
Rnds 2 and 4: [P2, k2] to end.

LACE PENNANT PATTERN

Repeat all 14 rnds once.

Rnd 1: [K6, ssk, yo] to end.
Rnd 2: [k7, p1] to end.
Rnd 3: [K5, ssk, yo, p1] to end.
Rnd 4: [K6, p2] to end.
Rnd 5: [K4, ssk, yo, p2] to end.
Rnd 6: [K5, p3] to end.
Rnd 7: [K3, ssk, yo, p3] to end.
Rnd 8: [K4, p4] to end.
Rnd 9: [K2, ssk, yo, p4] to end.
Rnd 10: [K3, p5] to end.
Rnd 11: [K1, ssk, yo, p5] to end.
Rnd 12: [K2, p6] to end.
Rnd 13: [Ssk, yo, p6] to end.
Rnd 14: [K1, p7] to end.

INSTRUCTIONS

Cuff

With MC, CO **56 (64, 72, 80)** sts and join for working in the rnd, being careful not to twist your sts. Est 2×2 ribbing: [k2, p2] to end.

Cont working ribbing until your Cuff measures 2" (5 cm).

Leg

Work Garter Ridge Border, then Double Moss Pattern, then Garter Ridge Border, then Lace Pennant Pattern, then Garter Ridge Border, then 2×2 Rib Pattern. Finish the Leg by knitting the Garter Ridge Border.

Note: If you would like to make your Leg longer or shorter, simply add or subtract pattern panels. I don't recommend stopping for the Heel in the middle of a panel as it will disrupt the symmetry of the panel lengths.

Heel Flap

Work the first rnd of the Double Moss Pattern across the first **28 (32, 36, 40)** sts, then begin working your Heel Flap back and forth across the remaining **28 (32, 36, 40)** sts as follows:

Row 1 (RS): K2, [slip 1, k1] to end. Turn work.

Row 2 (WS): Slip 1 wyif, purl to end. Turn work.

Row 3: [Slip 1, k1] to end. Turn work.

Repeat rows 2 and 3 until Heel Flap measures **2 (2, 2¼, 2½)" [5 (5, 6, 6.5) cm]**. End *after* you have worked row 3.

Heel Turn

Row 1 (WS): Slip 1 wyif, p**14 (16, 18, 20)**, p2tog, p1, turn.

Row 2 (RS): Slip 1, k3, ssk, k1, turn.

Row 3: Slip 1 wyif, p4, p2tog, p1, turn.

Row 4: Slip 1, k5, ssk, k1, turn.

You have now established the following pattern for your Heel Turn: Slip 1, knit or purl to 1 st before the gap created by turning on the previous row, ssk or p2tog, k1 or p1, turn. Cont in this pattern until all your Heel sts have been worked, ending on a RS row. You should now have **16 (18, 20, 22)** Heel sts.

Gusset

With the right side of your work facing, pick up and knit **12 (14, 16, 18)** sts along the left side of your Heel Flap.

Next, work in Double Moss Pattern (you should be on rnd 2) across the **28 (32, 36, 40)** sts that we've left undisturbed on our needles while working our Heel Flap. Pm, and pick up **12 (14, 16, 18)** sts on the right side of the Heel Flap. Knit across the Heel sts, then knit down the first set of new sts you picked up on the left side. You've reached the end of the rnd, and all your sts have now been picked up. You should now have **68 (78, 88, 98)** sts on your needles.

Gusset Decreases

Rnd 1: Work in current pattern panel across **28 (32, 36, 40)** sts, sl m, k1, ssk, knit around to 3 sts before the end of rnd, k2tog, k1.

Rnd 2: Work even with no decreases.

Repeat these 2 rnds until you have **56 (64, 72, 80)** sts on your needles.

Foot

Cont working the pattern panels in the order established on the Leg across the first **28 (32, 36, 40)** sts, and working Stockinette (knit every st) across the remaining **28 (32, 36, 40)** sts until your Foot reaches just to the tip of your pinky toe. Try to end after completing a pattern panel, but if this isn't possible, don't sweat it! Your sock will still look beautiful. If you can't easily try on your socks as you knit (working on double-pointed needles or tiny circulars can make this challenging), or if you are knitting gift socks for some lucky recipient, the Craft Yarn Council has issued the following length guidelines for the Foot of a sock, measured from the back of the Heel to the end of the Toe.

(All sizes are US.)
Women's shoe sizes 4–6.5: 8–9" (20.25–23 cm)
Women's shoe sizes 7–9.5: 9¼–10" (23.5–25.5 cm)
Women's shoe sizes 10–12.5: 10¼–11" (26–28 cm)
Men's shoe sizes 6–8.5: 9¼–10" (23.5–25.5 cm)
Men's shoe sizes 9–11.5: 10¼–11" (26–28 cm)
Men's shoe sizes 12–14: 11¼–12" (28.5–30.5 cm)

When working a Heel Flap and Gusset, you need to take into account your Toe length.

S: 1½" (4 cm)
M: 1½" (4 cm)
L: 1½" (4 cm)
XL: 1¾" (4 cm)

Now, take your desired Foot length, from the back of the Heel to the end of the Toe, and subtract your Toe measurement. For example, my desired Foot length is 9" (23 cm). I subtract my Toe (1½" [4 cm]) and that leaves me with 7½" (19 cm) I need to knit before starting my Toe decreases. Measure starting at the back of the Heel.

Toe

Cut MC, and with CC, work the following decrease pattern for the Toe:

Rnd 1: K1, ssk, k**22 (26, 30, 34)** sts, k2tog, k1, pm, k1, ssk, k**22 (26, 30, 34)** sts, k2tog, k1.

Rnd 2: Knit.

Rnd 3: K1, ssk, knit to 3 sts before next marker, k2tog, k1, sl m, k1, ssk, knit around to 3 sts before end of rnd, k2tog, k1.

Repeat rnds 2 and 3 until **24 (28, 32, 36)** sts remain.

Use Kitchener Stitch to close up your Toe.

Finishing

Weave in all your ends and block your socks.

The Fisherman Fade

The blanket nest

Ribbed socks are my absolute favorite. Throw in stripes or a good fade, make them oversized and extra cozy, and I could die happily, ensconced in my blanket nest like the redneck prairie queen that I am, surrounded by books, with *The Lord of the Rings* trilogy humming quietly in the background for good measure.

The Fisherman Fade Socks are *next level* ribbed socks. Knit in a classic half fisherman's rib, that genius construction perfected by the knitting masters of the Irish and Scottish coastal communities, these socks stretch, slouch, and hug like no other sock. Put them on, cancel all your plans, and retreat into your home with a plate of pizza rolls and that book you've been excited to read all day. You'll have no wants, you'll have no ambitions, you'll have no purpose in life other than to just exist, happily, like a laird in his seaside castle. Let the wind batter the walls and the rain trample your garden. You are quite content with what the world may hurl your way, because you have the most perfect pair of ribbed socks.

DIFFICULTY LEVEL

Beginner

SKILLS

Knitting into the stitch below
Heel flap and gusset

MATERIALS

Yarn

Hedgehog Fibres Sock [90% superwash merino/10% nylon; 437 yards (400 m); 3½ ounces (100 g)]: (46) 58 (72, 88, 102) yards [(42) 53 (66, 80, 93) m] in Fly (MC)

Hedgehog Fibres Sock: (46) 58 (72, 88, 102) yards [(42) 53 (66, 80, 93) m] in Dreamy Club OOAK (one-of-a-kind) (CC1)

Hedgehog Fibres Sock: (22) 29 (36, 45, 52) yards [(20) 27 (33, 41, 48) m] in Brights Club OOAK (CC2)

Needles

US size 1 (2.25 mm)

Notions

Measuring tape, stitch markers, snips, tapestry needle

GAUGE

38 sts = 4" (10 cm), knit in Half Fisherman's Rib Pattern in the round and blocked

SIZES

(Kid) S (M, L, XL)

MEASUREMENTS

The numbers below refer to the circumference of the ball of the foot, not the measurements of the finished sock.

(5–6) 7 (8, 9, 10)" [(13–15) 18 (20, 23, 25) cm]

HALF FISHERMAN'S RIB PATTERN

Rnd 1: Knit.
Rnd 2: [K1below, p1] to end.

INSTRUCTIONS

Cuff

With MC, CO **(48) 56 (64, 72, 80)** sts and join for working in the rnd, being careful not to twist your sts. Est 1×1 ribbing: [k1, p1] to end.

Cont working the ribbing until your Cuff measures ¾" (2 cm), or your desired length.

Leg

Begin working the Half Fisherman's Rib Pattern. Cont working in MC until your Leg (including Cuff) measures 6" (15 cm), then begin fading in CC1 by working the following fade pattern *while continuing to work the Half Fisherman's Rib Pattern*: MC, CC1, MC, CC1, CC1, MC, MC, CC1, MC, CC1, CC1, MC. Repeat that pattern once more, then cont working the rest of the Leg in CC1. Stop for the Heel once the Leg (including Cuff) measures 7½" (19 cm).

Note: You can begin fading in your second color at any point in the Leg. If you'd prefer a longer or shorter Leg, simply start fading sooner or later than what I suggested above.

Heel Flap

Work in pattern across the first **(24) 28 (32, 36, 40)** sts, then begin working your Heel Flap back and forth across the remaining **(24) 28 (32, 36, 40)** sts as follows:

Row 1 (RS): K2, [slip 1, k1] to end. Turn work.

Row 2 (WS): Slip 1 wyif, purl to end. Turn work.

Row 3: [Slip 1, k1] to end. Turn work.

Repeat rows 2 and 3 until Heel Flap measures **(1¾) 2 (2, 2¼, 2½)" [(4.5) 5 (5, 6, 6.5) cm]**. End *after* you have worked row 3.

Heel Turn

Row 1 (WS): Slip 1 wyif, p**(12) 14 (16, 18, 20)**, p2tog, p1, turn.

Row 2 (RS): Slip 1, k3, ssk, k1, turn.

Row 3: Slip 1 wyif, p4, p2tog, p1, turn.

Row 4: Slip 1, k5, ssk, k1, turn.

You have now established the following pattern for your Heel Turn: Slip 1, knit or purl to 1 st before the gap created by turning on the previous row, ssk or p2tog, k1 or p1, turn. Cont in this pattern until all your Heel sts have been worked, ending on a RS row. You should now have **(14) 16 (18, 20, 22)** Heel sts.

Gusset

With the right side of your work facing, pick up and knit **(10) 12 (14, 16, 18)** sts along the left side of your Heel Flap.

Next, work in pattern across the **(24) 28 (32, 36, 40)** sts that we've left undisturbed on our needles while working our Heel Flap. Pm, and pick up **(10) 12 (14, 16, 18)** sts on the right side of the Heel Flap. Knit across the Heel sts, then knit down the first set of new sts you picked up on the left side. You've reached the end of the rnd, and all your sts have now been picked up. You should now have **(58) 68 (78, 88, 98)** sts on your needles.

Gusset Decreases

Rnd 1: Work in pattern across **(24) 28 (32, 36, 40)** sts, sl m, k1, ssk, knit around to 3 sts before the end of rnd, k2tog, k1.

Rnd 2: Work even with no decreases.

Repeat these 2 rnds until you have **(48) 56 (64, 72, 80)** sts on your needles.

Foot

Cont working in Half Fisherman's Rib Pattern across the first **(24) 28 (32, 36, 40)** sts, and working Stockinette (knit every st) across the remaining **(24) 28 (32, 36, 40)** sts until you are ready to fade in CC2. I began fading once my Foot reached the middle of the arch of my foot, which was approximately 2½" (6 cm) beyond the end of my Gusset Decreases. Follow the same fade pattern you used on the Leg *while at the same time* continuing to work the Half Fisherman's Rib Pattern across the first **(24) 28 (32, 36, 40)** sts, and working Stockinette across the remaining **(24) 28 (32, 36, 40)** sts.

Cont working with CC2 until your Foot reaches just to the tip of your pinky toe. If you can't easily try on your socks as you knit (working on double-pointed needles or tiny circulars can make this challenging), or if you are knitting gift socks for some lucky recipient, the Craft Yarn Council has issued the following length guidelines for the Foot of a sock, measured from the back of the Heel to the end of the Toe.

(All sizes are US.)
Kid: 6–7½" (15–19 cm)
Women's shoe sizes 4–6.5: 8–9" (20.25–23 cm)
Women's shoe sizes 7–9.5: 9¼–10" (23.5–25.5 cm)
Women's shoe sizes 10–12.5: 10¼–11" (26–28 cm)
Men's shoe sizes 6–8.5: 9¼–10" (23.5–25.5 cm)
Men's shoe sizes 9–11.5: 10¼–11" (26–28 cm)
Men's shoe sizes 12–14: 11¼–12" (28.5–30.5 cm)

When working a Heel Flap and Gusset, you need to take into account your Toe length.

Kid: 1¼" (3 cm)
S: 1½" (4 cm)
M: 1½" (4 cm)
L: 1½" (4 cm)
XL: 1¾" (4 cm)

Now, take your desired Foot length, from the back of the Heel to the end of the Toe, and subtract your Toe measurement. For example, my desired Foot length is 9" (23 cm). I subtract my Toe (1½" [4 cm]) and that leaves me with 7½" (19 cm) I need to knit before starting my Toe decreases. Measure starting at the back of the Heel.

Toe

Rnd 1: K1, ssk, k**(18) 22 (26, 30, 34)**, k2tog, k1, pm, k1, ssk, k**(18) 22 (26, 30, 34)**, k2tog, k1.

Rnd 2: Knit.

Rnd 3: K1, ssk, knit to 3 sts before next marker, k2tog, k1, sl m, k1, ssk, knit around to 3 sts before end of rnd, k2tog, k1.

Repeat rnds 2 and 3 until **(20) 24 (28, 32, 36)** sts remain.

Use Kitchener Stitch to close up your Toe.

Finishing

Weave in all your ends and block your socks.

Chapter 2

MODERN ART SOCKS

Growing up in rural Oklahoma didn't afford me access to museums or great works of art. (There is a different, though no less meaningful, poetry, however, in having hitching posts stationed at the post office so you can tie your horse up while you get the mail.) My only access to the works of Wassily Kandinsky, Vincent van Gogh, Frida Kahlo, Hilma af Klint, the Dutch masters, and Andrew Wyeth was through books and magazines at the library.

Frankly, it was tough to comprehend these two-dimensional photocopies printed on paper. Objectively they were nice to look at, but why would I stare at them for hours when I could be reading the Stephen King book hidden in my backpack? Words and stories, feelings explored through language—*that's* what moved my angsty little teenage self.

But then I grew up and moved to the Big City (big for Oklahoma at least), and I visited a museum and saw great works of art in person, and I got it. *I got it.* A giant canvas layered with paint, three inches in front of your face, pushes the feeling right up and out of you, like you've been hit with a sandbag right in the center of your chest. It's the texture, it's the form, it's all that radiant color! Which, incidentally, is what gets me so jazzed about sock knitting.

In this chapter I wanted to focus on creating patterns that use *color* to speak, though shapes and texture are explored as well. It is my hope that these patterns will inspire you to abandon what you *should* do with color, and instead think about what you *could* do. We're always so worried about what looks good to others. Am I doing this right? Did I pick the wrong combination? Will this look ugly?

I say get all that out of your system. Let's focus on what feels good and right to *ourselves*. If the colors end up looking blah or downright awful, we only have to rip back and try again, refining our own sense of color harmony in the process.

Color-Block Socks

I'd love to tell you that these socks, inspired by the work of Mark Rothko and Paul Klee, have some deep meaning, that the boxes represent the metaphorical boxes we put each other in, and the explosive color represents the uniqueness inside of us that is just dying to get out. But in reality, these socks were just a hoot and half to knit, and I thought of nothing but color fun when I designed them.

To be honest, I don't totally get Mark Rothko and Paul Klee. I love looking at their art, but I have no idea what they were trying to *say* with it, and I think that stops a lot of us from appreciating art because we don't know if we're appreciating it the "right" way. I've said this numerous times at workshops and speaking events (Yes, believe it or not, sock knitters get hired to speak to people about sock knitting. And yes, these events are absolutely wild!): There is no "right" way when it comes to making or viewing art.

Color selection is often primal—we choose a palette based on what we're feeling, often in the moment. And we return to favorite palettes time and time again. And those favorites change and evolve as *we* change and evolve.

Sometimes people bring me cake at sock knitting events. (Thanks, Amber!)

When knitting these socks, try a little experiment: Don't fret too much over which colors to pair together. Go by instinct. Go by feel. Go by your innate sense of what is right for you and you alone. I think you'll be surprised by and happy with the color story that unfolds with each completed round.

DIFFICULTY LEVEL

Advanced beginner

SKILLS

Stranded knitting
Afterthought heel

MATERIALS

Yarn

My friends, this is a true stash-busting project. I used so many little odds and ends with no labels that I couldn't begin to tell you colors or brands. But I can give you the base color and the amount of yarn you'll need, and that's something, right?

Hedgehog Fibres Sock [90% superwash merino/10% nylon; 437 yards (400 m); 3½ ounces (100 g)]: (56) 68 (82, 98, 116) yards [(51) 62 (75, 90, 106) m] (MC)

CC colors: You'll need a total of (38) 51 (67, 74, 90) yards [(35) 47 (61, 68, 82) m] of fingering weight sock yarn, divided however you see fit between the colors you use.

Needles

US size 1 (2.25 mm)
US size 2 (2.75 mm)

Notions

Measuring tape, stitch markers (including a clasp marker), snips, tapestry needle

GAUGE

36 sts = 4" (10 cm), knit in colorwork pattern in the round on US size 2 (2.75 mm) needles and blocked

SIZES

(Kid) S (M, L, XL)

MEASUREMENTS

The numbers below refer to the circumference of the ball of the foot, not the measurements of the finished sock.

(5–6) 7 (8, 9, 10)" [(13–15) 18 (20, 23, 25) cm]

COLOR-BLOCK CHART

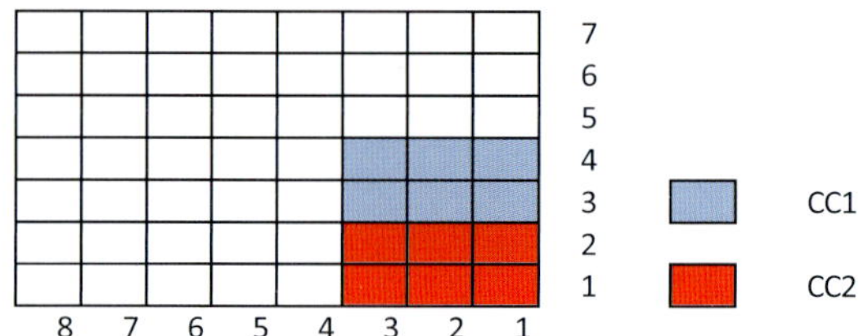

INSTRUCTIONS

Cuff

With MC and US size 1 (2.25 mm) needles, CO **(48) 57 (63, 72, 81)** sts and join for working in the rnd, being careful not to twist your sts. Est 2×1 ribbing: [k2, p1] to end.

Cont working ribbing pattern until Cuff measures ¾" (2 cm), or your desired length.

Leg

Switch to US size 2 (2.75 mm) needles and work 1 rnd even in Stockinette (knit every stitch), making the following inc or dec according to your size:

Kid: No inc or dec. **48 sts.**
S: Work to last 3 sts, k2tog, k1. **56 sts.**
M: Work to last 2 sts, kfb, k1. **64 sts.**
L: No inc or dec. **72 sts.**
XL: Work to last 3 sts, k2tog, k1. **80 sts.**

Work 1 more rnd even in Stockinette.

Now the color fun begins! Begin working the Colorblock Chart. Repeat all 7 rnds until your Leg (including the Cuff) measures 6" (15 cm), or your desired length. Stop for the Heel placement *after* working rnd 5.

You can work each repeat of the chart in different colors, as I did, or keep it super graphic and cool by sticking with the same two-color combo all the way down the sock. (You'll definitely have fewer ends to weave in going that route, LOL.)

Placing the Marker for the Afterthought Heel

Once you've decided your Leg is long enough, on the next rnd (you should be on rnd 7 of the chart), simply knit **(36) 42 (48, 54, 60)** sts, and clip a clasp marker onto that last st you just knit. Then just keep knitting to the end of the rnd. You have now marked where your Afterthought Heel will eventually go, and you should now be ready to work rnd 1 of the chart.

Foot

Cont repeating all 7 rnds of the chart until your Foot reaches the desired length. The Craft Yarn Council has issued the following guidelines for the Foot of a sock, measured from the back of the Heel to the end of the Toe.

(All sizes are US.)
Kid: 6–7½" (15–19 cm)
Women's shoe sizes 4–6.5: 8–9" (20.25–23 cm)
Women's shoe sizes 7–9.5: 9¼–10" (23–25.5 cm)
Women's shoe sizes 10–12.5: 10¼–11" (26–28 cm)
Men's shoe sizes 6–8.5: 9¼–10" (23.5–25.5 cm)
Men's shoe sizes 9–11.5: 10¼–11" (26–28 cm)
Men's shoe sizes 12–14: 11¼–12" (28.5–30.5 cm)

When working an Afterthought Heel, you need to take into account both your Heel length and your Toe length (they will be the same).

Kid: 1" (3 cm)
S: 1½" (4 cm)
M: 1½" (4 cm)
L: 1½" (4 cm)
XL: 1¾" (4 cm)

Now, take your desired Foot length, from the back of the Heel to the end of the Toe, and subtract both your Heel and Toe measurements. For example, my desired Foot length is 9" (23 cm). I subtract my Toe (1½" [4 cm]) and my Heel (1½" [4 cm]), and that leaves me with 6" (15 cm) I need to knit before starting my Toe decreases.

Toe

Break CC colors and switch back to US size 1 (2.25 mm) needles. Using MC, knit 1 rnd even in Stockinette, then begin the following decrease pattern to shape your Toe:

Rnd 1: K1, ssk, k **(18) 22 (26, 30, 34)** sts, k2tog, k1, pm, k1, ssk, k **(18) 22 (26, 30, 34)** sts, k2tog, k1.

Rnd 2: Knit.

Rnd 3: K1, ssk, knit to 3 sts before next marker, k2tog, k1, sl m, k1, ssk, knit around to 3 sts before end of rnd, k2tog, k1.

Repeat rnds 2 and 3 until **(20) 24 (28, 32, 36)** sts remain.

Use Kitchener Stitch to close up your Toe.

Knitting the Afterthought Heel

You should have a long tube with a Cuff at one end and a Toe at the other end. Go to the point in your tube where you placed the clasp marker. Make sure your tube is pressed flat. You should have half your sts facing up at you and the other half of your sts facing down. Your Toe should look like a wedge, with the decrease lines on the sides of the wedge.

Identify the line of sts directly below the clasp marker. Select the first st at the edge of your tube. With US size 1 (2.25 mm) needles, insert the needle into the right leg of that first st. Next, insert the needle into the right leg of the second st, and then into the right leg of the third st. Cont inserting your needle into the right leg of every st until you have picked up **(24) 28 (32, 36, 40)** sts. Next, repeat that process for the line of sts on the other side of your waste yarn. You should have **(48) 56 (64, 72, 80)** sts total divided evenly on your needles.

Remove the marker and tease that st up with your tapestry needle. Snip that st, being very careful not to snip anything else! Use your tapestry needle to tease out the yarn you've snipped from the sts. Start in the middle and go to the end on either side of your snipped st.

You now have a gaping hole in your sock tube and live Heel sts on the needles, ready to be worked. You also have a strand of yarn dangling on each side of the hole. Those will come in handy later when you weave in your ends. I use them to close gaps at the corners of the Heel.

Join in MC and knit 2 rnds even in Stockinette, then begin the following decrease pattern for your Heel:

Rnd 1: K1, ssk, k **(18) 22 (26, 30, 34)** sts, k2tog, k1, pm, k1, ssk, k **(18) 22 (26, 30, 34)** sts, k2tog, k1.

Rnd 2: Knit.

Rnd 3: K1, ssk, knit to 3 sts before next marker, k2tog, k1, sl m, k1, ssk, knit around to 3 sts before end of rnd, k2tog, k1.

Repeat rnds 2 and 3 until **(20) 24 (28, 32, 36)** sts remain.

Note: You can adjust the depth and fit of your Heel by working more or fewer decrease rnds. Try the sock on occasionally as you work your decreases to see how it's fitting. Stop your decreases when you can easily pinch the fabric closed.

Use Kitchener Stitch to close up your Heel.

Finishing

Weave in all your ends and block your socks.

Twisted Trellis Socks

The Boston Avenue Methodist Church in Tulsa, Oklahoma, is a world-famous example of Art Deco architecture and a perpetual font of design inspiration.

Socks that incorporate Art Deco cables, paired with not-so-boring beige and heightened with a surprise zing of neon at the toe, are a prime example of the intersection of art and craft.

I've said many times that I love a good tonal for expressing a cable story. How better to view those artfully twisted stitches than through the lens of a solid, even boring color? And what could be more boring than beige? And yet, I've come to discover that beige is actually quite thrilling in its very blandness.

My beige awakening happened a few years ago when I happened upon a color called Silence at my local yarn store. Produced by Hedgehog Fibres in County Cork, Ireland, this wondrous little skein of near colorless yarn made its way across the ocean to Oklahoma, where it hung on a little peg, waiting for me to find it.

I walked by it, then doubled back and took a second look. That beige, so ordinary, was calling my name. Look at me, it announced, barely above a whisper. I can do great things!

And when paired with a neon, it absolutely could. Add a little zing of bright yellow or pink at the cuff or toe, and that beige isn't beige any longer, it is a chic renaissance yarn, announcing itself boldly through its subtlety.

The razor-thin lines of this particular cable stitch were inspired by the Art Deco architecture Tulsa is famous for.

Once the oil capital of the world, Tulsa was flush with money, and its oil baron citizens built *lavishly*.

DIFFICULTY LEVEL

Intermediate

SKILLS

Twisted ribbing
Knitting through the back loop
Cable knitting
Heel flap and gusset

MATERIALS

Yarn

Hedgehog Fibres Sock [90% superwash merino/10% nylon; 437 yards (400 m); 3½ ounces (100 g)]: 182 (209, 232, 261) yards [166 (191, 212, 239) m] in Silence (MC)
Hedgehog Fibres Sock: 32 (36, 40, 44) yards [29 (33, 37, 40) m] in UFO (CC)

Needles

US size 1 (2.25 mm) needles

Notions

Measuring tape, stitch markers, snips, tapestry needle

GAUGE

38 sts = 4" (10 cm), knit in Twisted Trellis Cable Pattern on US size 2 (2.75mm) needles in the round and blocked

SIZES

S (M, L, XL)

MEASUREMENTS

The numbers below refer to the circumference of the ball of the foot, not the measurements of the finished sock.

7 (8, 9, 10)" [18 (20, 23, 25) cm]

TWISTED TRELLIS CABLE PATTERN CHART

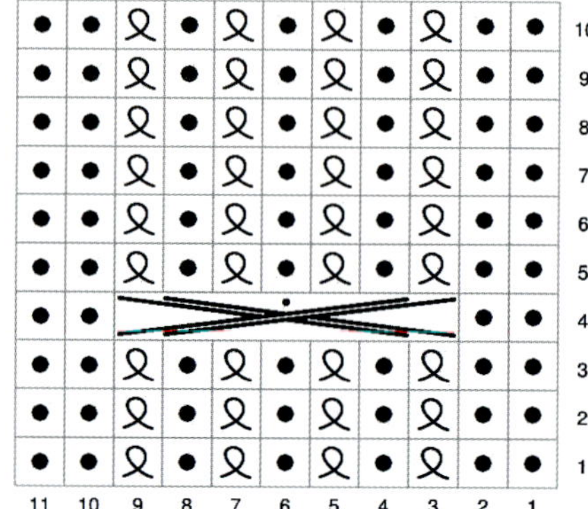

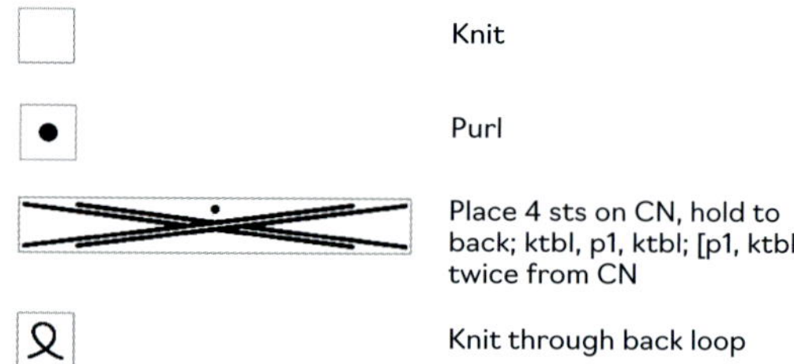

TWISTED TRELLIS CABLE PATTERN WRITTEN INSTRUCTIONS

Rnds 1, 2, 4–10: P2, [ktbl, p1] 3 times, ktbl, p2.

Rnd 3: P2, place 4 sts on CN, hold to back; ktbl, p1, ktbl; [p1, ktbl] twice from CN, p2.

INSTRUCTIONS

The Twisted Trellis Cable Pattern runs in a vertical band down the right side of the right sock, and down the left side of the left sock, meaning the instructions are slightly different for each sock.

Cuff

With MC, CO **56 (64, 72, 80)** sts and join for working in the rnd, being careful not to twist your sts. Est 1×1 twisted ribbing: [ktbl, ptbl] to end.

Cont working ribbing pattern until Cuff measures ¾" (2 cm), or your desired length.

Leg (Right Sock)

The Twisted Trellis Cable Pattern is only worked across the first 11 sts of your sock, with the rest of the round being Stockinette. Begin working your vertical cable band like so:
Work the first 11 sts in rnd 1 of the Twisted Trellis Cable Pattern, then work the remaining **45 (53, 61, 69)** sts in Stockinette.

Cont repeating all 10 rnds of the cable pattern over the first 11 sts of the sock, and knitting Stockinette on the remaining **45 (53, 61, 69)** sts until your Leg (including Cuff) measures 5" (13 cm), or your desired length. You can end on any rnd of the cable pattern.

Leg (Left Sock)

Work in Stockinette across the first **17 (21, 25, 29)** sts, work the 11 sts of the first rnd of the Twisted Trellis Cable Pattern, then work the remaining **28 (32, 36, 40)** sts in Stockinette.
Cont repeating all 10 rnds of this est pattern:
Work Stockinette across the first **17 (21, 25, 29)** sts, work the 11 sts of the Twisted Trellis Cable Pattern, then work the remaining **28 (32, 36, 40)** sts in Stockinette.

Once your Leg (including Cuff) measures 5" (13 cm), or your desired length, stop for the Heel.

Heel Flap

With CC, work in est Twisted Trellis Cable Pattern and Stockinette across the first **28 (32, 36, 40)** sts, then begin working your Heel Flap back and forth across the remaining **28 (32, 36, 40)** sts as follows:

Row 1 (RS): K2, [slip 1, k1] to end. Turn work.

Row 2 (WS): Slip 1 wyif, purl to end. Turn work.

Row 3: [Slip 1, k1] to end. Turn work.

Repeat rows 2 and 3 until Heel Flap measures **2 (2, 2¼, 2½)" [5 (5, 6, 6.5) cm]**. End *after* you have worked row 3.

Heel Turn

Row 1 (WS): Slip 1 wyif, p**14 (16, 18, 20)**, p2tog, p1, turn.

Row 2 (RS): Slip 1, k3, ssk, k1, turn.

Row 3: Slip 1 wyif, p4, p2tog, p1, turn.

Row 4: Slip 1, k5, ssk, k1, turn.

You have now established the following pattern for your Heel Turn: Slip 1, knit or purl to 1 st before the gap created by turning on the previous row, ssk or p2tog, k1 or p1, turn. Cont in this pattern until all your Heel sts have been worked, ending on a RS row. You should now have **16 (18, 20, 22)** Heel sts. Cut CC.

Gusset

With MC and the right side of your work facing, pick up and knit **12 (14, 16, 18)** sts along the left side of your Heel Flap.

Next, work in est Twisted Trellis Cable Pattern and Stockinette across the **28 (32, 36, 40)** sts that we've left undisturbed on our needles while working our Heel Flap. Pm, and pick up **12 (14, 16, 18)** sts on the right side of the Heel Flap. Knit across the Heel sts, then knit down the first set of new sts you picked up on the left side. You've reached the end of the rnd, and all your sts have now been picked up. You should now have **68 (78, 88, 98)** sts on your needles.

Gusset Decreases

Rnd 1: Work in est Twisted Trellis Cable Pattern and Stockinette across **28 (32, 36, 40)** sts, sl m, k1, ssk, knit around to 3 sts before the end of rnd, k2tog, k1.

Rnd 2: Work even with no decreases.

Repeat these 2 rnds until you have **56 (64, 72, 80)** sts on your needles.

Foot

Cont working in est Twisted Trellis Cable Pattern and Stockinette across the first **28 (32, 36, 40)** sts and working Stockinette across the remaining **28 (32, 36, 40)** sts until your Foot reaches just to the tip of your pinky toe. If you can't easily try on your socks as you knit (working on double-pointed needles or tiny circulars can make this challenging), or if you are knitting gift socks for some lucky recipient, the Craft Yarn Council has issued the following length guidelines for the Foot of a sock, measured from the back of the Heel to the end of the Toe.

(All sizes are US.)

Women's shoe sizes 4–6.5: 8–9" (20.25–23 cm)
Women's shoe sizes 7–9.5: 9¼–10" (23.5–25.5 cm)
Women's shoe sizes 10–12.5: 10¼–11" (26–28 cm)
Men's shoe sizes 6–8.5: 9¼–10" (23.5–25.5 cm)
Men's shoe sizes 9–11.5: 10¼–11" (26–28 cm)
Men's shoe sizes 12–14: 11¼–12" (28.5–30.5 cm)

When working a Heel Flap and Gusset, you need to take into account your Toe length.

S: 1½" (4 cm)
M: 1½" (4 cm)
L: 1½" (4 cm)
XL: 1¾" (4 cm)

Now, take your desired Foot length, from the back of the Heel to the end of the Toe, and subtract your Toe measurement. For example, my desired Foot length is 9" (23 cm). I subtract my Toe (1½" [4 cm]) and that leaves me with 7½" (19 cm) I need to knit before starting my Toe decreases. Measure starting at the back of the Heel.

Toe

Cut MC, join in CC, and begin the following decrease pattern for your Toes:

Rnd 1: K1, ssk, k **22 (26, 30, 34)** sts, k2tog, k1, pm, k1, ssk, k **22 (26, 30, 34)** sts, k2tog, k1.

Rnd 2: Knit.

Rnd 3: K1, ssk, knit to 3 sts before next marker, k2tog, k1, sl m, k1, ssk, knit around to 3 sts before end of rnd, k2tog, k1.

Repeat rnds 2 and 3 until **24 (28, 32, 36)** sts remain.

Use Kitchener Stitch to close up your Toe.

Finishing

Weave in all your ends and block your socks.

Escher Socks

I'm always on the lookout for art books at used bookstores! They provide endless inspiration for new designs.

These optical illusion socks were inspired by the work of Maurits Cornelis Escher, a Dutch genius who combined math and art to create extraordinary works that challenge the viewer's perception of reality. He played around with gravity, shape, and form in his work, engaging viewers in a wondrous world that was close to our own, but just different enough to throw us for a loop.

Shape and form can be explored through sock knitting as well. Yes, socks are generally foot-shaped, but can the fabric appear three-dimensional? Using colorwork, these socks give the illusion of blocks rising from the surface, a series of skyscrapers packed close together in a dense city center. I used a fun color-changing yarn for this pair, but working with two solid colors would be just as striking.

DIFFICULTY LEVEL

Intermediate

SKILLS

Stranded knitting
Forethought heel

MATERIALS

Yarn

Laines du Nord Watercolor Sock [75% superwash wool/25% nylon; 438 yards (400 m), 3½ ounces (100 g)]: (173) 198 (224, 252, 273) yards [(158) 181 (205, 230, 250) m] in 102 Rainbow (MC)

Cascade Heritage [75% superwash merino/ 25% nylon; 437 yards (400 m); 3½ ounces (100 g)]: (21) 24 (27, 30, 33) yards [(19) 22 (25, 27, 30) m] in 5682 White (CC)

Needles

US Size 1 (2.25 mm)
US Size 2 (2.75 mm)

Notions

Measuring tape, stitch markers, snips, tapestry needle, 24" (61 cm) length of waste yarn

GAUGE

36 sts = 4" (10 cm) and 28 rows, knit in Escher Chart pattern on US size 2 (2.75 mm) needles in the round and blocked.

SIZES

(Kid) S (M, L, XL)

MEASUREMENTS

The numbers below refer to the circumference of the ball of the foot, not the measurements of the finished sock.

(5–6) 7 (8, 9, 10)" [(13–15) 18 (20, 23, 25) cm]

ESCHER CHART

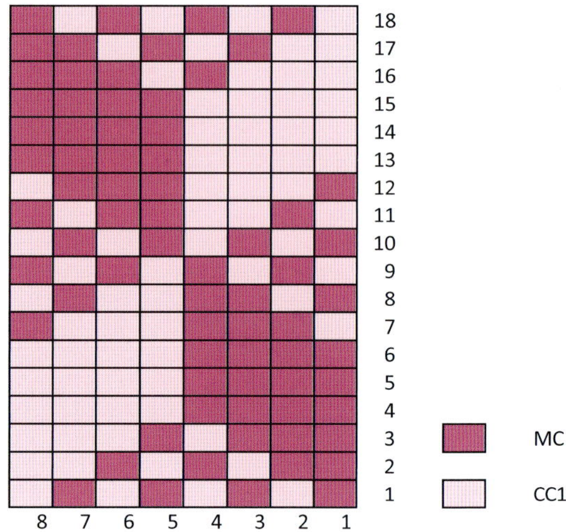

INSTRUCTIONS

Cuff

With MC and US Size 1 (2.25 mm) needles, CO **(48) 57 (63, 72, 81)** sts and join for working in the rnd, being careful not to twist your sts. Establish 2×1 ribbing: [k2, p1] to end.

Cont working the ribbing until your Cuff measures ¾" (2 cm), or your desired length. On the last rnd of the ribbing, we need to get our stitch count back to an even number. If you are working sizes **Kid** or **L**, you already have an even number and can move on to the Leg instructions. The rest of you, make the following increase or decrease according to your size:

S: Work in rib pattern to the last 3 sts, k2tog, p1. **56 sts.**

M: Work in rib pattern to the last 3 sts, kfb, k1, p1. **64 sts.**

XL: Work in rib pattern to the last 3 sts, k2tog, p1. **80 sts.**

Leg

Switch to US size 2 (2.75 mm) needles and begin working the Escher Chart. Repeat all 18 rnds of the chart until your Leg (including Cuff) measures 3" (8 cm), or your desired length. Stop for the Heel *after* working rnd 3.

Placing the Waste Yarn for the Forethought Heel

Work rnd 4 of the Escher Chart across the first **(24) 28 (32, 36, 40)** sts. Next, work the remaining **(24) 28 (32, 36, 40)** sts in a strand of waste yarn. Finally, transfer those **(24) 28 (32, 36, 40)** sts you just knit in your waste yarn from your right-hand needle back to your left-hand needle. Cont working rnd 4 of the Chart across those waste yarn sts you just transferred back to your left needle. You have now knit a strand of waste yarn where your Forethought Heel will eventually go.

Foot

Cont repeating all 18 rnds of the chart (you should be on rnd 5 now) until your Foot reaches the desired length. The Craft Yarn Council has issued the following guidelines for the Foot of a sock, measured from the back of the Heel to the end of the Toe.

(All sizes are US.)
Kid: 6–7½" (15–19 cm)
Women's shoe sizes 4–6.5: 8–9" (20.25–23 cm)
Women's shoe sizes 7–9.5: 9¼–10" (23.5–25.5 cm)
Women's shoe sizes 10–12.5: 10¼–11" (26–28 cm)
Men's shoe sizes 6–8.5: 9¼–10" (23.5–25.5 cm)
Men's shoe sizes 9–11.5: 10¼–11" (26–28 cm)
Men's shoe sizes 12–14: 11¼–12" (28.5–30.5 cm)

When working a Forethought Heel, you need to take into account both your Heel length and your Toe length (they will be the same).

Kid: 1¼" (3 cm)
S: 1½" (4 cm)
M: 1½" (4 cm)
L: 1½" (4 cm)
XL: 1¾" (4 cm)

Now, take your desired Foot length, from the back of the Heel to end of the Toe, and subtract both your Heel and Toe measurements. For example, my desired Foot length is 9" (23 cm). I subtract my Toe (1½" [4 cm]) and my Heel (1½" [4 cm]) and that leaves me with 6" (15 cm) I need to knit before starting my Toe decreases.

Toes

Switch to US size 1 (2.25 mm) needles and begin the following decrease pattern for your Toes:

Rnd 1: K1, ssk, k**(18) 22 (26, 30, 34)** sts, k2tog, k1, pm, k1, ssk, k**(18) 22 (26, 30, 34)** sts, k2tog, k1.

Rnd 2: Knit.

Rnd 3: K1, ssk, knit to 3 sts before next marker, k2tog, k1, sl m, k1, ssk, knit around to 3 sts before end of rnd, k2tog, k1.

Repeat rnds 2 and 3 until **(20) 24 (28, 32, 36)** sts remain.

Graft your Toe closed using Kitchener Stitch.

Knitting the Forethought Heel

You should have a long tube with a Cuff at one end and a Toe at the other end. Go to the point in your tube where you knit in that line of waste yarn. Make sure your tube is pressed flat. You should have half your sts facing up at you and the other half of your sts facing down. Your Toe should look like a wedge, with the decrease lines on the sides of the wedge.

Identify the line of sts directly below the waste yarn. Select the first st directly below the first waste line st. With US size 1 (2.25 mm) needles, insert the tip of your needle into the right leg of that first st. Next, insert the needle into the right leg of the second st, and then into the right leg of the third st. Cont inserting your needle into the right leg of every st until you have picked up **(24) 28 (32, 36, 40)** sts. Next, repeat that process for the line of sts on the other side of the waste yarn. You should now have **(48) 56 (64, 72, 80)** sts on your needles ready to be knit.

Join in CC and knit 2 rnds even in Stockinette, then begin the following decrease pattern for your Heel:

Rnd 1: K1, ssk, k**(18) 22 (26, 30, 34)** sts, k2tog, k1, pm, k1, ssk, k**(18) 22 (26, 30, 34)** sts, k2tog, k1.

Rnd 2: Knit.

Rnd 3: K1, ssk, knit to 3 sts before next marker, k2tog, k1, sl m, k1, ssk, knit around to 3 sts before end of rnd, k2tog, k1.

Repeat rnds 2 and 3 until **(20) 24 (28, 32, 36)** sts remain.

Note: You can adjust the depth and fit of your Heel by working more or fewer decrease rnds. Try the sock on occasionally as you work your decreases to see how it's fitting. Stop your decreases when you can easily pinch the fabric closed.

Use Kitchener Stitch to close up your Heel.

Finishing

Weave in all your ends and block your socks.

Studio Socks

I am obsessed with photographs of artists at work in their studios. I've always been intensely curious about the way other people live, the furnishings they choose, the books they read, the clothes they wear, the routines they follow. Our homes and work spaces are such a reflection of who we are, so getting a peek into how a creative lives and works gives us insight into their process.

I think all of us artists, to some degree, are a little insecure about our own processes. Are we doing it right? Could we produce better work if we did it like someone else? There's always a human compulsion to compare, which can both serve us and destroy us. Compare yourself to who you were last year? Productive! Compare yourself to the artist who has been working twenty years longer than you? Madness!

And yet, I think there is inspiration to be had in looking at how other artists do their work, in their intimate spaces. Even if my space looks nothing like Georgia O'Keeffe's studio, I feel inspired to create *something* just by poring over photographs of where she lived and created.

My "studio" is just my spot on the couch.

The Studio Socks were designed with an artist at work in mind. A vintage, feminine lace pattern paired with bold colors and playful stripes at the toes feels like the space a modern artist inhabits—finding new ways to interpret what has been done before.

DIFFICULTY LEVEL

Beginner

SKILLS

Yarn overs

Decrease stitches

Heel flap and gusset

MATERIALS

Yarn

Plucky Knitter Primo Fingering Sock [75% superwash merino/20% cashmere/5% nylon; 440 yards (402 m); 4 ounces (115 g)]: 165 (189, 211, 234) yards [151 (173, 193, 214) m] in Zinc Oxide (MC)

La Bien Aimée Super Sock [75% superwash merino/25% nylon; 465 yards (425 m); 3½ ounces (100 g)]: 21 (26, 29, 34) yards [19 (24, 27, 31) m] in Seaglass (CC1)

La Bien Aimée Super Sock: 8 (10, 12, 14) yards [7 (9, 11, 13) m] in Jonna (CC2)

Coates & Co. Cottage Sock [75% superwash merino wool/25% nylon; 437 yards (400 m); 3½ ounces (100 g)]: 7 (9, 11, 13) yards [6 (8, 10, 12) m] in Color No. 13 Pistachio (CC3)

Needles

US size 1 (2.25 mm)

Notions

Measuring tape, stitch markers, snips, tapestry needle

GAUGE

38 sts = 4" (10 cm), knit in Diamond Lace Pattern on US size 1 (2.25mm) needles in the round and blocked

SIZES

S (M, L, XL)

MEASUREMENTS

The numbers below refer to the circumference of the ball of the foot, not the measurements of the finished sock.

7 (8, 9, 10)" [18 (20, 23, 25) cm]

DIAMOND LACE CHART

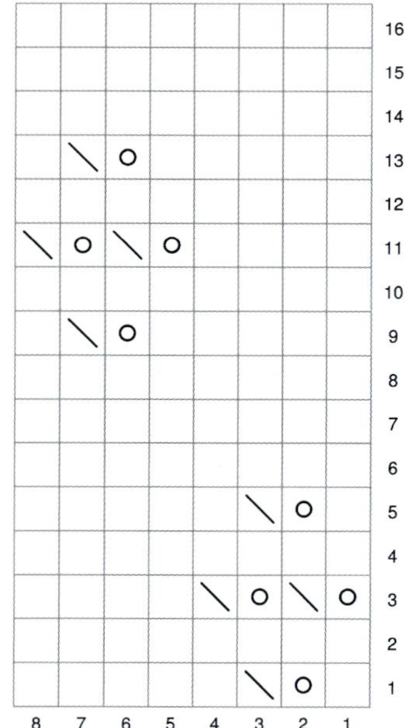

INSTRUCTIONS

Cuff

With CC1, CO **56 (64, 72, 80)** sts and join for working in the rnd, being careful not to twist your sts. Est 2×2 rib pattern: [k2, p2] to end.

Cont working ribbing until Cuff measures 3" (8 cm) or your desired length. Break CC1.

Leg

Join in MC and work 2 rnds even in Stockinette (knit every st). Next, begin working the Diamond Lace Chart. Repeat all 16 rnds of the Chart until Leg measures 7" (18 cm), or your desired length. End *after* working a rnd 6 or 14.

Heel Flap

Work in Diamond Lace Pattern across the first **28 (32, 36, 40)** sts, then begin working your Heel Flap back and forth across the remaining **28 (32, 36, 40)** sts as follows:

Row 1 (RS): K2, [slip 1, k1] to end. Turn work.

Row 2 (WS): Slip 1 wyif, purl to end. Turn work.

Row 3: [Slip 1, k1] to end. Turn work.

Repeat rows 2 and 3 until Heel Flap measures **2 (2, 2¼, 2½)" [5 (5, 6, 6.5) cm]**. End *after* you have worked row 3.

Heel Turn

Row 1 (WS): Slip 1 wyif, p**14 (16, 18, 20)**, p2tog, p1, turn.

Row 2 (RS): Slip 1, k3, ssk, k1, turn.

Row 3: Slip 1 wyif, p4, p2tog, p1, turn.

Row 4: Slip 1, k5, ssk, k1, turn.

You have now established the following pattern for your Heel Turn: Slip 1, knit or purl to 1 st before the gap created by turning on the previous row, ssk or p2tog, k1 or p1, turn. Cont in this pattern until all your Heel sts have been worked, ending on a RS row. You should now have **16 (18, 20, 22)** Heel sts.

Gusset

With the right side of your work facing, pick up and knit **12 (14, 16, 18)** sts along the left side of your Heel Flap.

Next, work in Diamond Lace Pattern across the **28 (32, 36, 40)** sts that we've left undisturbed on our needles while working our Heel Flap. Pm, and pick up **12 (14, 16, 18)** sts on the right side of the Heel Flap. Knit across the Heel sts, then knit down the first set of new sts you picked up on the left side. You've reached the end of the rnd, and all your sts have now been picked up. You should now have **68 (78, 88, 98)** sts on your needles.

Gusset Decreases

Rnd 1: Work in Diamond Lace Pattern across **28 (32, 36, 40)** sts, sl m, k1, ssk, knit around to 3 sts before the end of rnd, k2tog, k1.

Rnd 2: Work even with no decreases.

Repeat these 2 rnds until you have **56 (64, 72, 80)** sts on your needles.

Foot

Cont repeating all 16 rnds of the Diamond Lace Pattern across the first **28 (32, 36, 40)** sts and working Stockinette (knit every st) across the remaining **28 (32, 36, 40)** sts until your Foot reaches just to the tip of your pinky toe. If you can't easily try on your socks as you knit (working on double-pointed needles or tiny circulars can make this challenging), or if you are knitting gift socks for some lucky recipient, the Craft Yarn Council has issued the following length guidelines for the Foot of a sock, measured from the back of the Heel to the end of the Toe.

(All sizes are US.)
Women's shoe sizes 4–6.5: 8–9" (20.25–23 cm)
Women's shoe sizes 7–9.5: 9¼–10" (23.5–25.5 cm)
Women's shoe sizes 10–12.5: 10¼–11" (26–28 cm)
Men's shoe sizes 6–8.5: 9¼–10" (23.5–25.5 cm)
Men's shoe sizes 9–11.5: 10¼–11" (26–28 cm)
Men's shoe sizes 12–14: 11¼–12" (28.5–30.5 cm)

When working a Heel Flap and Gusset, you need to take into account your Toe length.

S: 1½" (4 cm)
M: 1½" (4 cm)
L: 1½" (4 cm)
XL: 1¾" (4 cm)

Now, take your desired Foot length, from the back of the Heel to the end of the Toe, and subtract your Toe measurement. For example, my desired Foot length is 9" (23 cm). I subtract my Toe (1½" [4 cm]) and that leaves me with 7½" (19 cm) I need to knit before starting my Toe decreases. Measure starting at the back of the Heel.

Toe

Break MC and join in CC2. Work rnd even in Stockinette, then begin working the decrease pattern for the Toe. *At the same time* work the following stripe pattern as you work the Toe decreases: [2 rnds CC2, 2 rnds CC3] to end.

Rnd 1: K1, ssk, k**22 (26, 30, 34)** sts, k2tog, k1, pm, k1, ssk, k**22 (26, 30, 34)** sts, k2tog, k1.

Rnd 2: Knit.

Rnd 3: K1, ssk, knit to 3 sts before next marker, k2tog, k1, sl m, k1, ssk, knit around to 3 sts before end of rnd, k2tog, k1.

Repeat rnds 2 and 3 until **24 (28, 32, 36)** sts remain.

Use Kitchener Stitch to close up your Toe.

Finishing

Weave in all your ends and block your socks.

Impressionist Socks

Now is the time for our speckled and variegated yarns to shine! This pattern introduces **marling** into our vocabulary, a technique that involves holding two different yarn strands together. When used with speckled or variegated yarns, the effect is quite painterly. Two fingering weight yarns held together equal a DK weight yarn, so we'll be using larger needles for this pair. I think you'll love how quickly they knit up, and how fun it is to create your own impressionist-style fabric by pairing hand-dyed yarns together.

Some Marling Tips

I like to choose similar colors when marling. In this pair, I chose a bold pink-and-orange variegated yarn held together with a lighter pink speckled yarn. You can also mix a neutral speckle (where the dominant base color is a beige, white, or gray) with a colorful speckled yarn, where turquoise, pink, blue, orange, and so on form the base for the speckles.

Where the yarns sit on your finger impacts which color will show up the most in the stitch. The strand that sits to the left will dominate the strand that sits to the right. This won't be much of an issue with colors that are similar, or when pairing a neutral with a color. But if you are pairing two very different colors, like an orange variegated and a turquoise variegated, you'll want to pay attention to which strand is on the left so you can mix it up every few stitches or rounds. This will give you an even mix of the colors.

DIFFICULTY LEVEL

Beginner

SKILLS

Marling yarn
Cable knitting
Heel flap and gusset

MATERIALS

Yarn

Hedgehog Fibres Sock [90% superwash merino/10% nylon; 437 yards (400 m); 3½ ounces (100 g)]: 104 (129, 146, 171) yards [95 (118, 134, 156) m] in OOAK (one-of-a-kind) (A)

Hedgehog Fibres Sock: 104 (129, 146, 171) yards [95 (118, 134, 156) m] in OOAK (B)

Needles

US size 3 (3.25 mm)

Notions

Measuring tape, stitch markers, snips, tapestry needle

GAUGE

28 sts = 4" (10 cm), knit in Cable Pattern on US size 3 (3.25 mm) needles in the round and blocked

SIZES

S (M, L, XL)

MEASUREMENTS

The numbers below refer to the circumference of the ball of the foot, not the measurements of the finished sock.

7 (8, 9, 10)" [18 (20, 23, 25) cm]

CABLE CHART

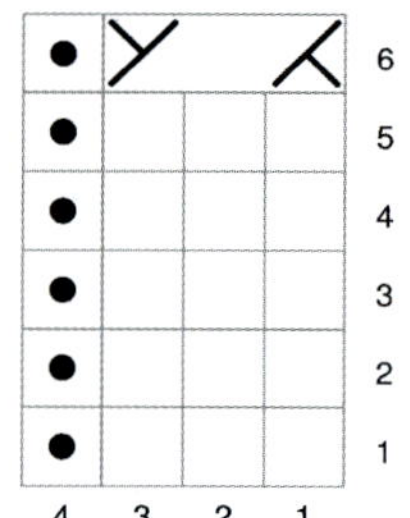

Knit

Purl

Sl 1 st to CN and hold to back; k2, k1 from CN

CABLE WRITTEN INSTRUCTIONS

Rnds 1–5: [K3, p1] to end.

Rnd 6: [Sl 1 to CN and hold in back, k2, k1 from CN, p1] to end.

INSTRUCTIONS

Leg

With yarns A and B held together, CO **40 (48, 56, 64)** sts and join for working in the rnd, being careful not to twist your sts. Begin Cable Pattern. Cont working all 6 rnds of the Cable Chart until Leg measures 5½" (14 cm) or your desired length. You can stop for the Heel on any rnd of the chart.

Heel Flap

Work in Cable Pattern across the first **20 (24, 28, 32)** sts, then begin working your Heel Flap back and forth across the remaining **20 (24, 28, 32)** sts as follows:

Row 1 (RS): K2, [slip 1, k1] to end. Turn work.

Row 2 (WS): Slip 1 wyif, purl to end. Turn work.

Row 3: [Slip 1, k1] to end. Turn work.

Repeat rows 2 and 3 until Heel Flap measures **2 (2, 2¼, 2½)" [5 (5, 6, 6.5) cm]**. End *after* you have worked row 3.

Heel Turn

Row 1 (WS): Slip 1 wyif, p**10 (12, 14, 16)**, p2tog, p1, turn.

Row 2 (RS): Slip 1, k3, ssk, k1, turn.

Row 3: Slip 1 wyif, p4, p2tog, p1, turn.

Row 4: Slip 1, k5, ssk, k1, turn.

You have now established the following pattern for your Heel Turn: Slip 1, knit or purl to 1 st before the gap created by turning on the previous row, ssk or p2tog, k1 or p1, turn. Cont in this pattern until all your Heel sts have been worked, ending on a RS row. You should now have **12 (14, 16, 18)** Heel sts.

Gusset

With the right side of your work facing, pick up and knit **8 (8, 8, 10)** sts along the left side of your Heel Flap.

Next, work in Cable Pattern across the **20 (24, 28, 32)** sts that we've left undisturbed on our needles while working our Heel Flap. Pm, and pick up **8 (8, 8, 10)** sts on the right side of the Heel Flap. Knit across the Heel sts, then knit down the first set of new sts you picked up on the left side. You've reached the end of the rnd, and all your sts have now been picked up. You should now have **48 (54, 60, 70)** sts on your needles.

Gusset Decreases

Rnd 1: Work in Cable Pattern across **20 (24, 28, 32)** sts, sl m, k1, ssk, knit around to 3 sts before the end of rnd, k2tog, k1.

Rnd 2: Work even with no decreases.

Repeat these 2 rnds until you have **40 (48, 56, 64)** sts on your needles.

Foot

Cont repeating all 6 rnds of the Cable Pattern across the first **20 (24, 28, 32)** sts and working Stockinette (knit every st) across the remaining **20 (24, 28, 32)** sts until your Foot reaches just to the tip of your pinky toe. If you can't easily try on your socks as you knit (working on double-pointed needles or tiny circulars can make this challenging), or if you are knitting gift socks for some lucky recipient, the Craft Yarn Council has issued the following length guidelines for the Foot of a sock, measured from the back of the Heel to the end of the Toe.

(All sizes are US.)
Women's shoe sizes 4–6.5: 8–9" (20.25–23 cm)
Women's shoe sizes 7–9.5: 9¼–10" (23.5–25.5 cm)
Women's shoe sizes 10–12.5: 10¼–11" (26–28 cm)
Men's shoe sizes 6–8.5: 9¼–10" (23.5–25.5 cm)
Men's shoe sizes 9–11.5: 10¼–11" (26–28 cm)
Men's shoe sizes 12–14: 11¼–12" (28.5–30.5 cm)

When working a Heel Flap and Gusset, you need to take into account your Toe length.

S: 1½" (4 cm)
M: 1½" (4 cm)
L: 1½" (4 cm)
XL: 1¾" (4 cm)

Now, take your desired Foot length, from the back of the Heel to the end of the Toe, and subtract your Toe measurement. For example, my desired Foot length is 9" (23 cm). I subtract my Toe (1½" [4 cm]) and that leaves me with 7½" (19 cm) I need to knit before starting my Toe decreases. Measure starting at the back of the Heel.

Toe

Work 1 rnd even in Stockinette, then begin working the decrease pattern for the Toe:

Rnd 1: K1, ssk, k**14 (18, 22, 26)** sts, k2tog, k1, pm, k1, ssk, k**14 (18, 22, 26)** sts, k2tog, k1.

Rnd 2: Knit.

Rnd 3: K1, ssk, knit to 3 sts before next marker, k2tog, k1, sl m, k1, ssk, knit around to 3 sts before end of rnd, k2tog, k1.

Repeat rnds 2 and 3 until **20 (24, 28, 32)** sts remain.

Use Kitchener Stitch to close up your Toe.

Finishing

Weave in all your ends and block your socks.

Chapter 3

EVERYDAY SOCKS

My favorite days are the ordinary ones. I don't look forward to events, outings, vacations, festivals, shopping excursions, or other forms of hullabaloo. I have to drag myself to any kind of planned frivolity. Once there, I usually enjoy myself (against my will), but it's the *anticipation* of a break in my routine that fills me with dread.

I like waking up knowing that this day will be exactly the same as the days before it. I will shower, take my kids to school, then take my dog on a walk that is precisely 2.32 miles. Once home, I will sit down to eat a breakfast of three egg bites and a protein shake while I read the news. From there, other domestic duties round out my early morning: emptying the clean dishes and loading the dirty ones, making the bed, rounding up towels from the teen bathrooms, fluffing the couch cushions, lighting the candles, and, in general, making my atmosphere conducive to work.

The rest of the day is a pleasant, homely hum of work, lunch, gym, school pickup, and evening reading. "Habitual" is one of my favorite words for a reason. I realize I sound like I've got a giant stick wedged up my backside, but order is necessary to temper the creative chaos inside my brain. Routine balances out the almost manic need to fly from one creative task to the next, barely taking a breath as I knit socks furiously into the night. I need a bedtime, is the simplest way to explain it, really.

I am also in need of reliable, comforting, soothing sock patterns to turn to time and again, when the weather is rough, so to speak, and my routines are shattered. When trips and holidays and deadlines loom, disrupting the natural sequence of my days, I need to knit socks that don't require too much thinking. I need to *wear* socks that are classic and comforting, not too loud, not too fussy, not too over-the-top.

The everyday socks in this chapter are the perfect antidote to busyness and chaos. They are the essence of simplicity, yet each pattern is interesting to knit. They go with everything and can be anything you need them to be. Perfect for repeat knitting, these patterns are a reliable stable of recipes you can pull from when more complex patterns are just *too much*.

Taking my teens to the local record store is one of my favorite everyday activities.

Lopi Sweater Socks

So beautiful, but so hot and itchy!

I still remember the moment I felt I'd really advanced as a knitter. I'd just completed a lopi sweater out of true Icelandic wool yarn, and it was nearly flawless. No puckering in my colorwork yoke, my underarm grafting was neat and tidy, and the fit was perfect. What beauty lay before me on my blocking mats! Once it dried, I put it on, then, after five tortuous minutes, ripped it right the hell off. It was *hot* hot. And the itch! Had I knit a sweater out of a thousand wasps?! *What was happening?*

It turns out, a hermit from Oklahoma who has never traveled beyond the borders of these United States knows very little about the composition and qualities of Icelandic wool. Yes, it's hot, because Iceland is very cold. Yes, it's itchy and coarse, because Icelandic sheep live outside in an unforgiving environment and their wool must protect them from the elements. Here I was, like a rube on a sunny, mild winter day, thinking I could pop on my new sweater and swan around town looking like an ad for a ski resort.

Oklahoma winters will almost never get cold enough to wear an Icelandic sweater, so that one beautiful lopi sweater will likely be the last I knit. But the design and spirit of a classic lopi can fortunately be translated onto a pair of soft merino socks. Knit up a half dozen pairs in a rainbow of colors, and you've got a classic, everyday staple that looks festive, cheery, and ski resort worthy for every day of the week.

DIFFICULTY LEVEL

Advanced beginner

SKILLS

Stranded colorwork

Heel flap and gusset

MATERIALS

Yarn

Cascade Heritage [75% superwash merino/ 25% nylon; 437 yards (400 m); 3½ ounces (100 g)]: (60) 78 (94, 113, 131) yards [71 (86, 103, 120) m] in 5752 Golden Yellow (MC)

Cascade Heritage: (30) 36 (42, 48, 54) yards [33 (38, 44, 49) m] in 5682 White (CC1)

Cascade Heritage: (20) 26 (32, 38, 44) [24 (29, 35, 40) m] in 5631 Charcoal (CC2)

Cascade Heritage: (4) 8 (12, 16, 20) yards [7 (11, 15, 18) m] in 5781 Clear Sky (CC3)

Needles

US size 1 (2.25 mm)

US size 2 (2.75 mm)

Notions

Measuring tape, stitch markers, snips, tapestry needle

GAUGE

32 sts = 4" (10 cm), knit in colorwork pattern on US size 2 (2.75 mm) needles in the round and blocked

SIZES

(Kid) S (M, L, XL)

MEASUREMENTS

The numbers below refer to the circumference of the ball of the foot, not the measurements of the finished sock.

(5–6) 7 (8, 9, 10)" [(13–15) 18 (20, 23, 25) cm]

LOPI SWEATER CHART

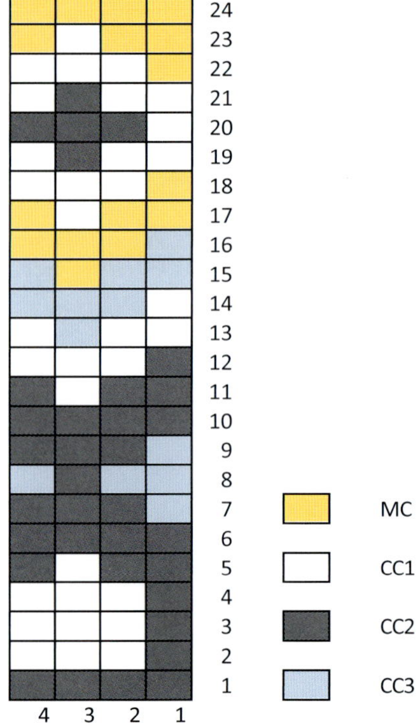

INSTRUCTIONS

Cuff

With MC, CO **(48) 56 (64, 72, 80)** sts and join for working in the rnd, being careful not to twist your sts. Work even in Stockinette (knit every st) for 4 rnds. Cut MC and join in CC1. Est 2×2 ribbing: [k2, p2] to end. Cont working 2×2 ribbing until entire Cuff measures 1.25" (3 cm), or your desired length. Do not cut CC1!

Leg

Join in CC2 and knit 1 rnd even in Stockinette, then begin working chart. Work all 24 rnds of the chart *once*. Break all CC colors and cont working in Stockinette with MC until Leg (including Cuff) measures 6" (15 cm), or your desired length.

Heel Flap

Knit across the first **(24) 28 (32, 36, 40)** sts, then begin working your Heel Flap back and forth across the remaining **(24) 28 (32, 36, 40)** sts as follows:

Row 1 (RS): K2, [slip 1, k1] to end. Turn work.

Row 2 (WS): Slip 1 wyif, purl to end. Turn work.

Row 3: [Slip 1, k1] to end. Turn work.

Repeat rows 2 and 3 until Heel Flap measures **(1¾) 2 (2, 2¼, 2½)" [(4) 5 (5, 6, 6.5) cm]**. End *after* you have worked row 3.

Heel Turn

Row 1 (WS): Slip 1 wyif, p **(12) 14 (16, 18, 20)** sts, p2tog, p1, turn.

Row 2 (RS): Slip 1, k3, ssk, k1, turn.

Row 3: Slip 1 wyif, p4, p2tog, p1, turn.

Row 4: Slip 1, k5, ssk, k1, turn.

You have now established the following pattern for your Heel Turn: Slip 1, knit or purl to 1 st before the gap created by turning on the previous row, ssk or p2tog, k1 or p1, turn. Cont in this pattern until all your Heel sts have been worked, ending on a RS row. You should now have **(14) 16 (18, 20, 22)** Heel sts. Cut CC.

Gusset

With the right side of your work facing, pick up and knit **(10) 12 (14, 16, 18)** sts along the left side of your Heel Flap.

Next, work across the **(24) 28 (32, 36, 40)** sts that you've left undisturbed on your needles while working our Heel Flap. Pm, and pick up **(10) 12 (14, 16, 18)** sts on the right side of the Heel Flap. Knit across the Heel sts, then knit down the first set of new sts you picked up on the left side. You've reached the end of the rnd, and all your sts have now been picked up. You should now have **(58) 68 (78, 88, 98)** sts on your needles.

Gusset Decreases

Rnd 1: Work across **(24) 28 (32, 36, 40)** sts, sl m, k1, ssk, knit around to 3 sts before the end of rnd, k2tog, k1.

Rnd 2: Work even with no decreases.

Repeat these 2 rnds until you have **(48) 56 (64, 72, 80)** sts on your needles.

Foot

Cont working in Stockinette until your Foot reaches just to the tip of your pinky toe. If you can't easily try on your socks as you knit (working on double-pointed needles or tiny circulars can make this challenging), or if you are knitting gift socks for some lucky recipient, the Craft Yarn Council has issued the following length guidelines for the Foot of a sock, measured from the back of the Heel to the end of the Toe.

(All sizes are US.)
Kid: 6–7½" (15–19 cm)
Women's shoe sizes 4–6.5: 8–9" (20.25–23 cm)
Women's shoe sizes 7–9.5: 9¼–10" (23.5–25.5 cm)
Women's shoe sizes 10–12.5: 10¼–11" (26–28 cm)
Men's shoe sizes 6–8.5: 9¼–10" (23.5–25.5 cm)
Men's shoe sizes 9–11.5: 10¼–11" (26–28 cm)
Men's shoe sizes 12–14: 11¼–12" (28.5–30.5 cm)

When working a Heel Flap and Gusset, you need to take into account your Toe length.

Kid: 1¼" (3 cm)
S: 1½" (4 cm)
M: 1½" (4 cm)
L: 1½" (4 cm)
XL: 1¾" (4 cm)

Now, take your desired Foot length, from the back of the Heel to the end of the Toe, and subtract your Toe measurement. For example, my desired Foot length is 9" (23 cm). I subtract my Toe (1½" [4 cm]) and that leaves me with 7½" (19 cm) I need to knit before starting my Toe decreases. Measure starting at the back of the Heel.

Toe

Begin the following decrease pattern for your Toes:

Rnd 1: K1, ssk, k**(18) 22 (26, 30, 34)** sts, k2tog, k1, pm, k1, ssk, k**(18) 22 (26, 30, 34)** sts, k2tog, k1.

Rnd 2: Knit.

Rnd 3: K1, ssk, knit to 3 sts before next marker, k2tog, k1, sl m, k1, ssk, knit around to 3 sts before end of rnd, k2tog, k1.

Repeat rnds 2 and 3 until **(20) 24 (28, 32, 36)** sts remain.

Use Kitchener Stitch to close up your Toe.

Finishing

Weave in all your ends and block your socks.

Flock Socks

I was a teenager in the 1990s, and my personal aesthetic was a small-town Oklahoma version of the grunge looks worn by my favorite bands. Did I have Doc Martens combat boots? No, I did not. But I did have secondhand Justin Roper boots. (Just google them—you'll die. They were lace-up cowgirl boots with FRINGE.) I wore them with jean shorts, a crocheted vest, and a bucket hat. This was my fourteen-year-old attempt at looking like Eddie Vedder, and it *did NOT eat*, as my teen daughter would say.

I, being a connoisseur of alternative bands like the Pixies, Rage Against the Machine, Nirvana, Radiohead, and Hole, rejected anything remotely preppy. I was too *cool*, too *cultured*, too tuned into the Seattle music scene (though I'm sure I had only a vague idea of where Seattle even *was*). I should also mention I was insufferable, LOL.

Now, sliding into my mid-forties, I've become obsessed with preppy outfits from the nineties. I look at old J.Crew catalogs for fun (seriously). Princess Diana running errands in bike shorts, an oversized sweatshirt, and scrunch socks? YES. JFK Jr. relaxing on his sailboat in a fisherman's sweater and faded jeans. PLEASE.

Teenage me,
trying to be grunge, with unfortunate bangs

The Flock Socks are my happy love letter to my current obsession with all things vintage preppy. The simple, sweet bird pattern makes me think of nineties New England college kids, sipping coffee and listening to Portishead on their Discmans between classes.

An easy knit, these are socks to make time and time again, changing up the color scheme depending on your mood. A perfect wardrobe staple for the fall and winter months, this timeless design will be a favorite of mine for years to come.

DIFFICULTY LEVEL

Beginner

SKILLS

Stranded colorwork
Striped ribbing
Afterthought heel

MATERIALS

Yarn

Option A

Knit Picks Stroll [75% fine superwash merino/ 25% nylon; 230 yards (211 m); 1¾ ounces (50 g)]: (104) 116 (128, 137, 151) yards [(95) 106 (117, 125, 138) m] in Jack Rabbit Heather (MC)

Knit Picks Stroll: (32) 49 (61, 88, 97) yards [(29) 45 (56, 80, 89) m] in Electric Blue (CC1)

Knit Picks Stroll: (28) 36 (47, 58, 66) yards [(26) 33 (43, 53, 60) m] in Goldenrod Heather (CC2)

Option B

Knit Picks Stroll: (104) 116 (128, 137, 151) yards [(95) 106 (117, 125, 138) m] in Cranberry Heather (MC)

Knit Picks Stroll: (32) 49 (61, 88, 97) yards [(29) 45 (56, 80, 89) m] in Pucker (CC1)

Knit Picks Stroll: (28) 36 (47, 58, 66) yards [(26) 33 (43, 53, 60) m] in Goldenrod Heather (CC2)

Needles

US size 1 (2.25 mm)
US size 2 (2.75 mm)

Notions

Measuring tape, stitch markers (including a clasp marker), snips, tapestry needle

GAUGE

32 sts = 4" (10 cm), knit in Flock Pattern on US size 2 (2.75 mm) needles in the rnd and blocked

SIZES

(Kid) S (M, L, XL)

MEASUREMENTS

The numbers below refer to the circumference of the ball of the foot, not the measurements of the finished sock.

(5–6) 7 (8, 9, 10)" [(13–15) 18 (20, 23, 25) cm]

FLOCK CHART

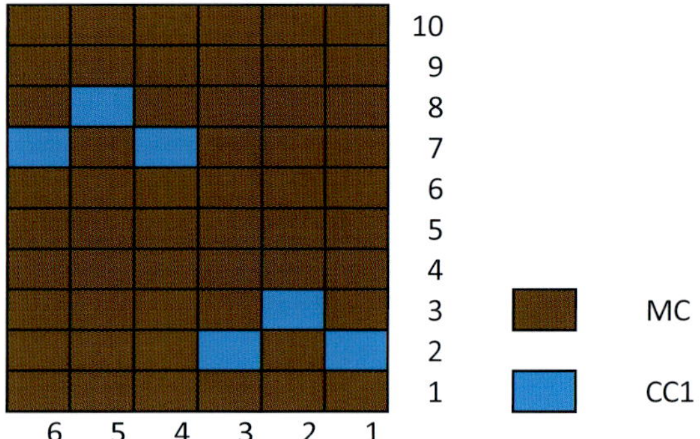

INSTRUCTIONS

Cuff

With US size 1 (2.25 mm) needles and MC, CO **(48) 54 (66, 72, 78)** sts and join for working in the rnd. Est 2×1 rib pattern: [k2, p1] to end.

Work 5 more rnds of ribbing in MC. Switch to CC1 and work 3 rnds. Next, work 6 rnds in MC, then 3 rnds in CC1, and finish with 6 rnds in MC. Don't cut either yarn strand! You'll need both for the Leg.

Leg

Work 1 rnd even in MC, then begin Flock Chart. Repeat all 10 rnds of the chart until your Leg (including Cuff) measures 6" (15 cm), or your desired length. End *after* working a rnd 4 or 9 of the chart.

Placing the Marker for the Afterthought Heel

Once your Leg is the appropriate length, on the next rnd, simply knit **(36) 40 (49, 54, 58)** sts and clip a clasp marker on that last st you just knit (you should be on rnd 5 or 10 of the Flock Chart). Then just keep knitting to the end of the rnd. You have now marked where your Afterthought Heel will eventually go.

Foot

Cont working the chart until your Foot reaches just to the tip of your pinky toe. If you can't easily try the sock on, or if you are knitting gift socks for some lucky recipient, the Craft Yarn Council has issued the following length guidelines for the Foot of a sock, measured from the back of the Heel to the end of the Toe.

(All sizes are US.)
Kid: 6–7½" (15–19 cm)
Women's shoe sizes 4–6.5: 8–9" (20.25–23 cm)
Women's shoe sizes 7–9.5: 9¼"–10" (23.5–25.5 cm)
Women's shoe sizes 10–12.5: 10¼–11" (26–28 cm)
Men's shoe sizes 6–8.5: 9¼–10" (23.5–25.5 cm)
Men's shoe sizes 9–11.5: 10¼–11" (26–28 cm)
Men's shoe sizes 12–14: 11¼–12" (28.5–30.5 cm)

When working an Afterthought Heel, you need to take into account both your Heel length and your Toe length (they will be the same).

Kid: 1" (3 cm)
S: 1½" (4 cm)
M: 1½" (4 cm)
L: 1½" (4 cm)
XL: 1¾" (4 cm)

Now, take your desired Foot length, from the back of the Heel to the end of the Toe, and subtract both your Heel and Toe measurements. For example, my desired Foot length is 9" (23 cm). I subtract my Toe (1½" [4 cm]) and my Heel (1½" [4 cm]) and that leaves me with 6" (15 cm) I need to knit before starting my Toe decreases. End *after* completing a rnd 4 or 9.

Sizes **S, M, XL** ONLY, work the following setup rnd prior to working the Toes:

S: K1, ssk, k25, k2tog, knit around to end. **52 sts.**
M: K1, ssk, k31, k2tog, knit around to end. **64 sts.**
XL: K1, ssk, k37, k2tog, knit around to end. **76 sts.**

Toe

Cut MC and CC1 and join in CC2. With US size 1 (2.25 mm) needles, work the following decrease rnds:

Rnd 1: K1, ssk, k**(18) 20 (26, 30, 32)** sts, k2tog, k1, pm, k1, ssk, k**(18) 20 (26, 30, 32)** sts, k2tog, k1.

Rnd 2: Knit.

Rnd 3: K1, ssk, knit to 3 sts before next marker, k2tog, k1, sl m, k1, ssk, knit around to 3 sts before end of rnd, k2tog, k1.

Repeat rnds 2 and 3 until **(20) 24 (28, 32, 36)** sts remain.

Use Kitchener Stitch to close the Toe.

Knitting the Afterthought Heel

You should have a long tube with a Cuff at one end, and a Toe at the other end. Go to the point in your tube where you placed the clasp marker. Make sure the tube is pressed flat. You should have half your sts facing up at you and the other half of your sts facing down. Your Toe should look like a wedge, with the decrease lines on the sides of the wedge.

Identify the line of stitches directly below the st you've marked with your clasp marker. Select the first st at the edge of your tube on that line of sts, and with US Size 1 (2.25 mm) needles, insert the tip of your needle into the right leg of that first st. Next, insert the needle into the right leg of the second st, and then into the right leg of the third st. Cont inserting your needle into the right leg of every st until you have picked up **(24) 28 (32, 36, 40)** sts.

Now, repeat that same process for the line of sts on the other side of your marked st. You should have **(48) 56 (64, 72, 80)** sts total divided evenly on your needles.

Remove the marker and tease that st up with your tapestry needle. Snip that st, being very careful not to snip anything else! Use your tapestry needle to tease out the yarn you've snipped from the sts. Start in the middle and go to the end on either side of your snipped st.

You now have a gaping hole in your sock tube and live Heel sts on the needles, ready to be worked. You also have a strand of yarn dangling on each side of the hole you've made. Those will come in handy later when you weave in your ends. I use them to close any gaps I get at the corner of the Heel.

You will work your Afterthought Heel the same as you did your Toe. Join in your yarn. Sizes **Kid** and **L**, work 3 rnds even in Stockinette, then move on to the Heel Decreases below.

Sizes **S, M, XL** ONLY, work the following setup rnd prior to working the Heel:

S: K1, ssk, k25, k2tog, knit around to end. **52 sts.**
M: K1, ssk, k31, k2tog, knit around to end. **64 sts.**
XL: K1, ssk, k37, k2tog, knit around to end. **76 sts.**

Work 2 more rnds even in Stockinette, then begin working the Heel Decreases.

Note: Try the sock on occasionally as you work. Once you can easily pinch the fabric closed around your Heel, stop doing decreases and close it up with Kitchener Stitch.

Rnd 1: K1, ssk, k**(18) 20 (26, 30, 32)** sts, k2tog, k1, pm, k1, ssk, k**(18) 20 (26, 30, 32)** sts, k2tog, k1. **4 sts decreased.**

Rnd 2: Knit.

Rnd 3: K1, ssk, knit to 3 sts before next marker, k2tog, k1, sl m, k1, ssk, knit around to 3 sts before end of rnd, k2tog, k1. **4 sts decreased.**

Repeat rnds 2 and 3 until **(20) 24 (28, 32, 36)** sts remain.

Use Kitchener Stitch to close the Heel.

Finishing

Weave in all your ends and block your socks.

Ribbed Trouser Socks

See, what did I tell you?
Subaru driver hiking aesthetic.

I should preface this pattern by telling you that I don't actually wear trousers. I don't work in an office or do anything remotely fancy, thus I never have occasion to wear something so grown-up as a pair of trousers that, in all likelihood, require dry cleaning. I wear jeans, jeans, sweatpants, flannel shirts, cargo pants, jeans, and more jeans. If I had to sum up my current wardrobe, I'd describe it as "Subaru owner who lives in the suburbs but still dresses as if a spontaneous mountain hike might happen at any moment."

It is my firm belief, however, that we all need some dressy pieces in our wardrobe, and that includes socks! The ribbing pattern on these socks is easy to knit. Usually I see ribbed socks and I automatically think of hiking boots and pajamas. But this particular pattern results in an elegant fabric that pairs well with loafers, or even cute clogs. You can knit them in a lightly speckled yarn, as I did, but I really think these socks would shine in a cool neon. Or, better yet, a neutral with neon heels and toes.

DIFFICULTY LEVEL

Beginner

SKILLS

Heel flap and gusset

MATERIALS

Yarn

Little Skein Cashmere Blend [70% superwash merino/20% cashmere/10% nylon; 420 yards (384 m)], 4 ounces (115 g)]: 221 (255, 283, 311) yards [202 (233, 259, 284) m] in Blue Moon

Notions

Measuring tape, stitch markers, snips, tapestry needle

Needles

US size 1 (2.25 mm)

GAUGE

38 sts = 4" (10 cm), knit in rib pattern on US size 1 (2.25 mm) needles in the rnd and blocked

SIZES

S (M, L, XL)

MEASUREMENTS

The numbers below refer to the circumference of the ball of the foot, not the measurements of the finished sock.

7 (8, 9, 10)" [18 (20, 23, 25) cm]

INSTRUCTIONS

Leg

CO **56 (64, 72, 80)** sts and join for working in the rnd, being careful not to twist your sts. Est ribbing pattern: [k2, p1, k4, p1] to end.

Cont working in ribbing pattern until Leg measures 6" (15 cm), or your desired length.

Heel Flap

Work in ribbing pattern across the first **28 (32, 36, 40)** sts, then work the Heel Flap back and forth across the remaining **28 (32, 36, 40)** sts as follows:

Row 1 (RS): K2, [slip 1, k1] to end. Turn work.

Row 2 (WS): Slip 1 wyif, purl to end. Turn work.

Row 3: [Slip 1, k1] to end. Turn work.

Repeat rows 2 and 3 until Heel Flap measures **2 (2, 2¼, 2½)" [5 (5, 6, 6.5) cm]**. End *after* you have worked row 3.

Heel Turn

Row 1 (WS): Slip 1 wyif, p**14 (16, 18, 20)**, p2tog, p1, turn.

Row 2 (RS): Slip 1, k3, ssk, k1, turn.

Row 3: Slip 1 wyif, p4, p2tog, p1, turn.

Row 4: Slip 1, k5, ssk, k1, turn.

You have now established the following pattern for your Heel Turn: Slip 1, knit or purl to 1 st before the gap created by turning on the previous row, ssk or p2tog, k1 or p1, turn. Cont in this pattern until all your Heel sts have been worked, ending on a RS row. You should now have **16 (18, 20, 22)** Heel sts.

Gusset

With the right side of your work facing, pick up and knit **12 (14, 16, 18)** sts along the left side of your Heel Flap.

Next, work in est ribbing pattern across the **28 (32, 36, 40)** sts that you've left undisturbed on your needles while working your Heel Flap. Pm, and pick up **12 (14, 16, 18)** sts on the right side of the Heel Flap. Knit across the Heel sts, then knit down the first set of new sts you picked up on the left side. You've reached the end of the rnd, and all your sts have now been picked up. You should now have **68 (78, 88, 98)** sts on your needles.

Gusset Decreases

Rnd 1: Work in est ribbing pattern across **28 (32, 36, 40)** sts, sl m, k1, ssk, knit around to 3 sts before the end of rnd, k2tog, k1.

Rnd 2: Work even with no decreases.

Repeat these 2 rnds until you have **56 (64, 72, 80)** sts on your needles.

Foot

Cont working in ribbing pattern across the first **28 (32, 36, 40)** sts and in Stockinette across the remaining **28 (32, 36, 40)** sts until your Foot reaches just to the tip of your pinky toe. If you can't easily try on your socks as you knit (working on double-pointed needles or tiny circulars can make this challenging), or if you are knitting gift socks for some lucky recipient, the Craft Yarn Council has issued the following length guidelines for the Foot of a sock, measured from the back of the Heel to the end of the Toe.

(All sizes are US.)

Women's shoe sizes 4–6.5: 8–9" (20.25–23 cm)
Women's shoe sizes 7–9.5: 9¼–10" (23.5–25.5 cm)
Women's shoe sizes 10–12.5: 10¼–11" (26–28 cm)
Men's shoe sizes 6–8.5: 9¼–10" (23–25.5 cm)
Men's shoe sizes 9–11.5: 10¼–11" (26–28 cm)
Men's shoe sizes 12–14: 11¼–12" (28.5–30.5 cm)

When working a Heel Flap and Gusset, you need to take into account your Toe length.

S: 1½" (4 cm)
M: 1½" (4 cm)
L: 1½" (4 cm)
XL: 1¾" (4 cm)

Now, take your desired Foot length, from the back of the Heel to the end of the Toe, and subtract your Toe measurement. For example, my desired Foot length is 9" (23 cm). I subtract my Toe (1½" [4 cm]) and that leaves me with 7½" (19 cm) I need to knit before starting my Toe decreases. Measure starting at the back of the Heel.

Toe

Begin the following decrease pattern for your Toes:

Rnd 1: K1, ssk, k**22 (26, 30, 34)** sts, k2tog, k1, pm, k1, ssk, k**22 (26, 30, 34)** sts, k2tog, k1.

Rnd 2: Knit.

Rnd 3: K1, ssk, knit to 3 sts before next marker, k2tog, k1, sl m, k1, ssk, knit around to 3 sts before end of rnd, k2tog, k1.

Repeat rnds 2 and 3 until **24 (28, 32, 36)** sts remain.

Use Kitchener Stitch to close up your Toe.

Finishing

Weave in all your ends and block your socks.

Broken Bow Socks

Most people think Oklahoma is a prairie, just an endless sea of grass and cows, peopled by farmers, American Indians, and devout Baptists. We have all of those things, but there's so much more! Oklahoma actually has one of the most diverse ecosystems in the United States. We have prairies, mesas, swamps, old-growth forests, and even an ancient mountain range. Visit north-central Oklahoma and you'll see miles of that famed prairie where the buffalo roamed. But travel to southeastern Oklahoma and you'll see a radically different landscape. Wild forestland, hills, valleys, and a complex network of rivers, lakes, and streams. You could truly disappear into the woods and never be seen again.

Broken Bow, in far southeastern Oklahoma, is one of my favorite places to vacation. We rent a cabin in the woods and spend our days exploring the Mountain Fork River, hiking in the Ouachita National Forest, and swimming in Broken Bow Lake near the Kiamichi Mountains. I function best when I'm outside, away from people, listening to bird chatter and unsettling animal noises. I like stars, quiet, and the sound wind makes as it courses through the trees—far away from the monotonous whooshing of cars flying down the interstate.

These socks were designed and knit while we stayed in Broken Bow during the last gasp of summer. It was late August, and the heat was extreme. That didn't stop me from sitting on the deck of our little cabin, sweating profusely, but refusing to go inside, my wool yarn a damp puddle in my lap as I fussed over the perfect classic cabled cabin socks I would want come winter.

Kayaking on the Mountain Fork River in Broken Bow. Not pictured: the enormous copperhead snake behind us that we were furiously paddling away from.

The Broken Bow Socks only have cables down the sides, with plenty of relaxing Stockinette in between, making them a great candidate for a repeat knit. I chose a classic cabin color palette of brown and red, but they'd look lovely in any combination you dream up. What a vibe to knit them in lightly speckled yarn with a fun pop of color on the toes.

DIFFICULTY LEVEL

Advanced beginner

SKILLS

Cable knitting

Heel flap and gusset

MATERIALS

Yarn

Knit Picks Stroll [75% fine superwash merino/ 25% nylon; 230 yards (211 m); 1¾ ounces (50 g)]: 219 (248, 276, 299) yards [200 (227, 252, 273) m] in Grizzly Heather (MC)

Knit Picks Stroll: 36 (42, 48, 54) yards [33 (38, 44, 49) m] in Buoy (CC)

Notions

Measuring tape, stitch markers, snips, tapestry needle

Needles

US size 1 (2.25 mm)

GAUGE

38 sts = 4" (10 cm), knit in Cable Pattern in the rnd and blocked

SIZES

S (M, L, XL)

MEASUREMENTS

The numbers below refer to the circumference of the ball of the foot, not the measurements of the finished sock.

7 (8, 9, 10)" [18 (20, 23, 25) cm]

CABLE CHART

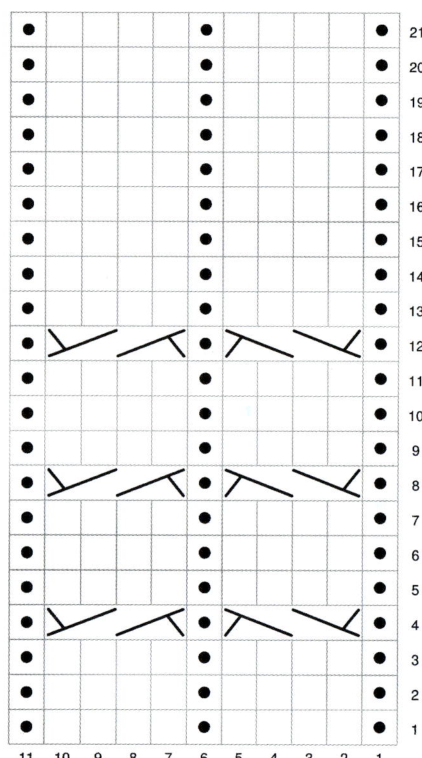

Knit

Purl

Slip 2 stitches to CN and hold in front; k2, k2 from CN

Slip 2 stitches to CN and hold in back; k2, k2 from CN

CABLE WRITTEN INSTRUCTIONS

C4F (Cable 4 Front): Sl 2 sts to CN and hold in front; k2, k2 from CN.

C4B (Cable 4 Back): Sl 2 sts to CN and hold in back; k2, k2 from CN.

Rnds 1–3, 5–7, 9–11, 13–21: P1, k4, p1, k4, p1.

Rnds 4, 8, 12: P1, C4F, p1, C4B, p1.

INSTRUCTIONS

Cuff

With US size 1 (2.25 mm) needles and MC, CO **57 (63, 72, 81)** sts and join for working in the rnd, being careful not to twist your sts. Begin the following ribbing and Cable Pattern:

Work rnd 1 of the Cable Chart over the first 11 sts, [k2, p1] **2 (3, 4, 6)** times, k2, work the Cable Chart over the next 11 sts, [k2, p1] to end.

Cont working each round of the Cable Chart along with the ribbing until your Cuff measures 1½" (4 cm), or your desired length.

Leg

We need to get our st counts back to normal, so work the following rnd *once* according to your size:

S: Work the Cable Chart over the first 11 sts, k1, k2tog, k5, work the Cable Chart over 11 sts, knit to end of rnd. **56 sts.**

M: Work the Cable Chart over the first 11 sts, k11, work the Cable Chart over 11 sts, k1, kfb, knit to end. **64 sts.**

L: Work the Cable Chart over the first 11 sts, k14, work the Cable Chart over 11 sts, knit to end. No increase or decrease. **72 sts.**

XL: Work the Cable Chart over the first 11 sts, k1, k2tog, k17, work the Cable Chart over 11 sts, knit to end. **80 sts.**

Cont repeating all 21 rnds of the Cable Chart in the following manner: Work the Cable Chart over the first 11 sts, k**8 (11, 14, 19)** sts, work the Cable Chart over 11 sts, knit to end.

Once your Leg has reached 6" (15 cm), or your desired length, stop for the Heel.

Heel Flap

Work in est Cable and Stockinette pattern across the first **28 (32, 36, 40)** sts, then, with CC, work the Heel Flap back and forth across the remaining **28 (32, 36, 40)** sts as follows:

Row 1 (RS): K2, [slip 1, k1] to end. Turn work.

Row 2 (WS): Slip 1 wyif, purl to end. Turn work.

Row 3: [Slip 1, k1] to end. Turn work.

Repeat rows 2 and 3 until Heel Flap measures **2 (2, 2¼, 2½)" [5 (5, 6, 6.5) cm]**. End *after* you have worked row 3.

Heel Turn

Row 1 (WS): Slip 1 wyif, p**14 (16, 18, 20)**, p2tog, p1, turn.

Row 2 (RS): Slip 1, k3, ssk, k1, turn.

Row 3: Slip 1 wyif, p4, p2tog, p1, turn.

Row 4: Slip 1, k5, ssk, k1, turn.

You have now established the following pattern for your Heel Turn: Slip 1, knit or purl to 1 st before the gap created by turning on the previous row, ssk or p2tog, k1 or p1, turn. Cont in this pattern until all your Heel sts have been worked, ending on a RS row. You should now have **16 (18, 20, 22)** Heel sts. Cut CC.

Gusset

With the right side of your work facing, pick up and knit **12 (14, 16, 18)** sts along the left side of your Heel Flap.

Next, work in est Cable and Stockinette pattern across the **28 (32, 36, 40)** sts that you've left undisturbed on your needles while working your Heel Flap. Pm, and pick up **12 (14, 16, 18)** sts on the right side of the Heel Flap. Knit across the Heel sts, then knit down the first set of new sts you picked up on the left side. You've reached the end of the rnd, and all your sts have now been picked up. You should now have **68 (78, 88, 98)** sts on your needles.

Gusset Decreases

Rnd 1: Work in est Cable and Stockinette pattern across **28 (32, 36, 40)** sts, sl m, k1, ssk, knit around to 3 sts before the end of rnd, k2tog, k1.

Rnd 2: Work even with no decreases.

Repeat these two rnds until you have **56 (64, 72, 80)** sts on your needles.

Foot

Cont working in Cable and Stockinette pattern across the first **28 (32, 36, 40)** sts and in Stockinette across the remaining **28 (32, 36, 40)** sts until your Foot reaches just to the tip of your pinky toe. If you can't easily try on your socks as you knit (working on double-pointed needles or tiny circulars can make this challenging), or if you are knitting gift socks for some lucky recipient, the Craft Yarn Council has issued the following length guidelines for the Foot of a sock, measured from the back of the Heel to the end of the Toe.

(All sizes are US.)

Women's shoe sizes 4–6.5: 8–9" (20.25–23 cm)
Women's shoe sizes 7–9.5: 9¼–10" (23.5–25.5 cm)
Women's shoe sizes 10–12.5: 10¼–11" (26–28 cm)
Men's shoe sizes 6–8.5: 9¼–10" (23.5–25.5 cm)
Men's shoe sizes 9–11.5: 10¼–11" (26–28 cm)
Men's shoe sizes 12–14: 11¼–12" (28.5–30.5 cm)

When working a Heel Flap and Gusset, you need to take into account your Toe length.

S: 1½" (4 cm)
M: 1½" (4 cm)
L: 1½" (4 cm)
XL: 1¾" (4 cm)

Now, take your desired Foot length, from the back of the Heel to the end of the Toe, and subtract your Toe measurement. For example, my desired Foot length is 9" (23 cm). I subtract my Toe (1½" [4 cm]) and that leaves me with 7½" (19 cm) I need to knit before starting my Toe decreases. Measure starting at the back of the Heel.

Toe

Begin the following decrease pattern for your Toes:

Rnd 1: K1, ssk, k**22 (26, 30, 34)** sts, k2tog, k1, pm, k1, ssk, k**22 (26, 30, 34)** sts, k2tog, k1.

Rnd 2: Knit.

Rnd 3: K1, ssk, knit to 3 sts before next marker, k2tog, k1, sl m, k1, ssk, knit around to 3 sts before end of rnd, k2tog, k1.

Repeat rnds 2 and 3 until **24 (28, 32, 36)** sts remain.

Use Kitchener Stitch to close up your Toe.

Finishing

Weave in all your ends and block your socks.

House Socks

One of the coolest experiences of my life was watching my son perform a Talking Heads song with his band on the stage at the Cain's Ballroom in downtown Tulsa while the actual members of the Talking Heads were in the audience.

I have no idea how or why they decided to attend a high school rock band performance (such a Talking Heads thing to do, honestly, just randomly showing up in nowhere Oklahoma for a night, only to disappear as quickly as they came). I was just standing there, jamming out awkwardly like the middle-aged mom with no rhythm that I am. I looked to my left, and there they were. Just casually watching *my* kid. It felt like a glitch in the matrix, a cosmic wink that we're living in a simulation.

These socks have nothing to do with that weird and wonderful night, but they *are* inspired by one of my favorite songs, which happens to be a Talking Heads song, "This Must Be the Place (Naive Melody)." "Home is where I want to be" is a phrase that calls my heart to harbor every time I hear it.

Ninety-nine percent of the time, I want to be home. I love home. Home is where I am safe and warm and the people I love are close by. Home is where all the books are, and where my spot on the couch is. My grandfather's coffee mug is here, and my plants too.

My son is the one on the right shredding the bass.

My grandmother's paintings are on the wall; my shoes are all lined up neatly in my closet; my favorite shampoo is sitting on the little ledge in my shower. Why would I ever want to leave?

The House Socks are the socks you put on when you get to be home. They are squishy and fuzzy and *right*. Designed with a classic texture stitch, they are interesting, but still relaxing to knit. Work them with a strand of mohair held together with sock yarn for extra luxury, or stick with a single strand of DK. Neutral colors, bright colors—it doesn't matter. Like all the timeless patterns in this chapter, these socks will look beautiful no matter how you personalize them.

DIFFICULTY LEVEL

Beginner

SKILLS

Heel flap and gusset

MATERIALS

Yarn

This is a DK weight sock pattern. I used a strand of fingering weight yarn held together with a strand of silk mohair yarn, but if you prefer, you can work with a single strand of DK yarn. Just follow the yardage recommendations for Yarn A.

Little Lionhead Knits Fingering Weight Soft Sock Yarn [85% superwash merino/15% nylon; 437 yards (400 m); 3½ ounces (100 g)]: 161 (180, 202, 224) yards [147 (164, 185, 205) m] in Forest Frolic (A)

Knitting for Olive Soft Silk Mohair [70% kid mohair/30% mulberry silk; 246 yards (225 m); 0.8 ounces (25 g)]: 161 (180, 202, 224) yards [147 (164, 185, 205) m] in Quince (B)

Needles

US size 3 (3.25 mm)

Notions

Measuring tape, stitch markers, snips, tapestry needle

GAUGE

28 sts = 4" (10 cm), knit in Texture Pattern on US size 3 (3.25 mm) needles in the round and blocked

SIZES

S (M, L, XL)

MEASUREMENTS

The numbers below refer to the circumference of the ball of the foot, not the measurements of the finished sock.

7 (8, 9, 10)" [18 (20, 23, 25) cm]

TEXTURE PATTERN CHART

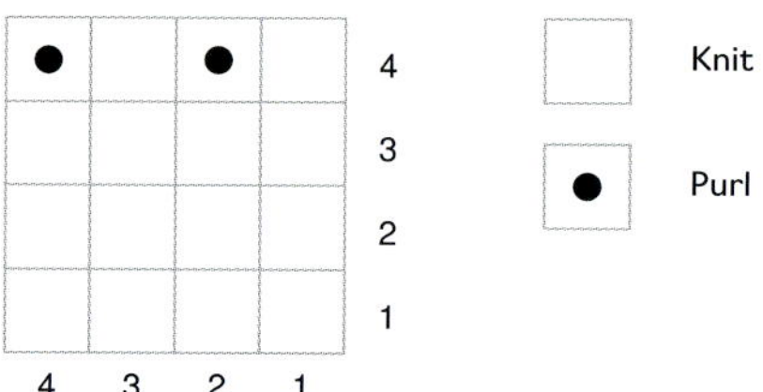

TEXTURE PATTERN WRITTEN INSTRUCTIONS

Rnds 1–3: Knit.

Rnd 4: [K1, p1] to end.

INSTRUCTIONS

Cuff

With yarns A and B held together (or with a single strand of DK yarn), CO **39 (48, 57, 63)** sts and join for working in the rnd, being careful not to twist your sts. Establish 2×1 ribbing pattern: [k2, p1] to end.

Cont working rib pattern until Cuff measures 1" (2.5 cm), or your desired length.

Leg

First, we need to get our stitch counts back to the normal DK weight sock numbers. Work 1 rnd of Stockinette, making the following adjustments according to your size:

S: Knit to last 2 sts, kfb, k1. **40 sts.**
M: Knit even. No inc or dec. **48 sts.**
L: Knit to last 3 sts, k2tog, k1. **56 sts.**
XL: Knit to last 2 sts, kfb, k1. **64 sts.**

Begin working the chart. Repeat all 4 rnds of the chart until the Leg, including Cuff, measures 5" (13 cm), or your desired length.

Heel Flap

Work in Texture Pattern across the first **20 (24, 28, 32)** sts, then begin working your Heel Flap back and forth across the remaining **20 (24, 28, 32)** sts as follows:

Row 1 (RS): K2, [slip 1, k1] to end. Turn work.

Row 2 (WS): Slip 1 wyif, purl to end. Turn work.

Row 3: [Slip 1, k1] to end. Turn work.

Repeat rows 2 and 3 until Heel Flap measures **2 (2, 2¼, 2½)" [5 (5, 6, 6.5) cm]**. End *after* you have worked row 3.

Heel Turn

Row 1 (WS): Slip 1 wyif, p**10 (12, 14, 16)**, p2tog, p1, turn.

Row 2 (RS): Slip 1, k3, ssk, k1, turn.

Row 3: Slip 1 wyif, p4, p2tog, p1, turn.

Row 4: Slip 1, k5, ssk, k1, turn.

You have now established the following pattern for your Heel Turn: Slip 1, knit or purl to 1 st before the gap created by turning on the previous row, ssk or p2tog, k1 or p1, turn. Cont in this pattern until all your Heel sts have been worked, ending on a RS row. You should now have **12 (14, 16, 18)** Heel sts.

Gusset

With the right side of your work facing, pick up and knit **8 (8, 8, 10)** sts along the left side of your Heel Flap.

Next, work in Texture Pattern across the **20 (24, 28, 32)** sts that you've left undisturbed on your needles while working your Heel Flap. Pm, and pick up **8 (8, 8, 10)** sts on the right side of the Heel Flap. Knit across the Heel sts, then knit down the first set of new sts you picked up on the left side. You've reached the end of the rnd, and all your sts have now been picked up. You should now have **48 (54, 60, 70)** sts on your needles.

Gusset Decreases

Rnd 1: Work in Texture Pattern across **20 (24, 28, 32)** sts, sl m, k1, ssk, knit around to 3 sts before the end of rnd, k2tog, k1.

Rnd 2: Work even with no decreases.

Repeat these 2 rnds until you have **40 (48, 56, 64)** sts on your needles.

Foot

Cont repeating all 4 rnds of the Texture Chart across the first **20 (24, 28, 32)** sts and working Stockinette (knit every st) across the remaining **20 (24, 28, 32)** sts until your Foot reaches just to the tip of your pinky toe. If you can't easily try on your socks as you knit (working on double-pointed needles or tiny circulars can make this challenging), or if you are knitting gift socks for some lucky recipient, the Craft Yarn Council has issued the following length guidelines for the Foot of a sock, measured from the back of the Heel to the end of the Toe.

(All sizes are US.)
Women's shoe sizes 4–6.5: 8–9" (20.25–23 cm)
Women's shoe sizes 7–9.5: 9¼–10" (23.5–25.5 cm)
Women's shoe sizes 10–12.5: 10¼–11" (26–28 cm)
Men's shoe sizes 6–8.5: 9¼–10" (23.5–25.5 cm)
Men's shoe sizes 9–11.5: 10¼–11" (26–28 cm)
Men's shoe sizes 12–14: 11¼–12" (28.5–30.5 cm)

When working a Heel Flap and Gusset, you need to take into account your Toe length.

S: 1½" (4 cm)
M: 1½" (4 cm)
L: 1½" (4 cm)
XL: 1¾" (4 cm)

Now, take your desired Foot length, from the back of the Heel to the end of the Toe, and subtract your Toe measurement. For example, my desired Foot length is 9" (23 cm). I subtract my Toe (1½" [4 cm]) and that leaves me with 7½" (19 cm) I need to knit before starting my Toe decreases. Measure starting at the back of the Heel.

Toe

Begin working the following decrease pattern for the Toe:

Rnd 1: K1, ssk, k**14 (18, 22, 26)** sts, k2tog, k1, pm, k1, ssk, k**14 (18, 22, 26)** sts, k2tog, k1.

Rnd 2: Knit.

Rnd 3: K1, ssk, knit to 3 sts before next marker, k2tog, k1, sl m, k1, ssk, knit around to 3 sts before end of rnd, k2tog, k1.

Repeat rnds 2 and 3 until **20 (24, 28, 32)** sts remain.

Use Kitchener Stitch to close up your Toe.

Finishing

Weave in all your ends and block your socks.

Chapter 4

WHIMSICAL SOCKS

There exists in my personal lore many specific obsessions: sock knitting (obviously), reading, being on time, empty cabinets (clutter = death), houseplants, lamp light, nuns (don't ask), mountain climbers, Radiohead's *OK Computer* album, Totino's Party Pizzas, and anything that is so over-the-top cute and whimsical it makes you just want to fall over and die because the cuteness has exploded your molecules.

This is the chapter I was most looking forward to creating, because colorwork socks featuring whimsical motifs are my absolute favorite to knit. (When I'm up for a fun time. If I'm tired, or mad at someone, or thinking too hard about that jackhammer sound the sun supposedly makes, then geez, give me a basic sock to knit, or a ribbed one at most.)

These designs are loaded with all my favorite cute things. There are fat little bees and mushrooms, sea crustaceans and sheep, and flowers (always flowers). Make them your own with your favorite colors (I see absolutely no reason why you can't knit your sheep out of hot pink yarn), and then wear them with Birkenstock sandals, because there is no better combination in my expert opinion that Birks and hand-knit socks.

Creating colorwork charts that operate on an eight-stitch repeat is always the most fuss-free. Sometimes to get a cute design, however, we might be working with a different stitch count. Such is the case for many of the patterns in this chapter. When different stitch counts are used outside of the norm, a pattern may call for specific sizes to use different needles than what you may be used to for colorwork. Be sure to read the instructions through before casting on so you can be sure you are working with the correct stitch counts and needle sizes.

A tiny portion of my houseplant collection

Forget-Me-Not Socks

Not pictured: forlorn cows

Winter in Oklahoma is a brown affair. We don't have many evergreen trees, so once the leaves go in autumn, the view outside our windows is rather depressing. There are no snow-capped mountains to admire or frigid ocean waves crashing against rocky shores. Just miles of brown sticks waving madly in the winter wind, the occasional cattle herd mooing forlornly in the distance.

Spring, however, makes up for our bland winter landscapes. The heat comes early (usually on the heels of a tornado outbreak), and the plants come ALIVE, swiftly and brilliantly, bursting out in a sudden onslaught of green, purple, red, yellow, and every other color on the spectrum. Spring, despite the violent weather, is what Oklahoma does best.

These socks are inspired by the vivid blue forget-me-not flowers I love so much. There's something so poignant about a tiny blue flower. I knit mine a bit larger than they appear in life, because bold, graphic flowers pop off of knitted socks.

DIFFICULTY LEVEL

Intermediate

SKILLS

Stranded knitting
Managing long floats
Afterthought heel

MATERIALS

Yarn

Cascade Heritage [75% superwash merino/ 25% nylon; 437 yards (400 m); 3½ ounces (100 g)]: 74 (92, 109, 131) yards [68 (84, 100, 120) m] in 5713 Placid Blue (MC)

Cascade Heritage: 52 (67, 80, 97) yards [48 (61, 73, 89) m] in 5615 Royal (CC1)

Cascade Heritage: 14 (18, 22, 26) yards [13 (16, 20, 24) m] in 5752 Golden Yellow (CC2)

Needles

US size 1 (2.25 mm)
US size 2 (2.75 mm)

Notions

Measuring tape, stitch markers (including a clasp marker), snips, tapestry needle

GAUGE

32 sts = 4" (10 cm), knit in colorwork pattern on US size 2 (2.75 mm) needles in the round and blocked

SIZES

S (M, L, XL)

MEASUREMENTS

The numbers below refer to the circumference of the ball of the foot, not the measurements of the finished sock.

7 (8, 9, 10)" [18 (20, 23, 25) cm]

FORGET-ME-NOT CHART

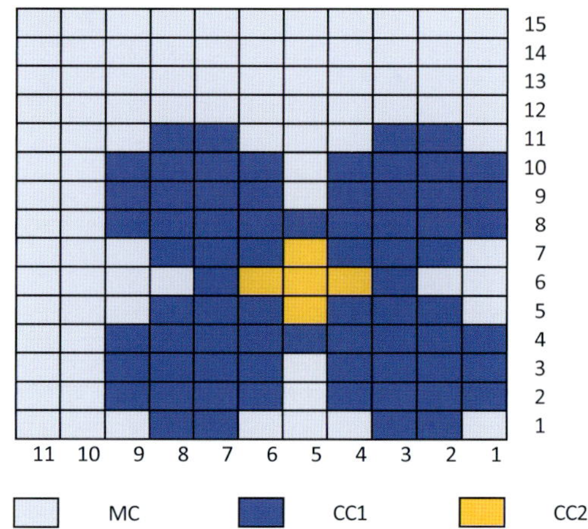

INSTRUCTIONS

Cuff

With MC and US size 1 (2.25 mm) needles, CO **54 (66, 78, 87)** sts and join for working in the rnd, being careful not to twist your sts. Est 2×1 ribbing: [k2, p1] to end.

Cont working the ribbing until your Cuff measures ¾" (2 cm), or your desired length. On the last rnd of the ribbing, we need to get our stitch count to the right amount for the chart. If you are working the size **M**, you already have the right number and can move on to the Leg instructions. The rest of you, make the following increase or decrease according to your size:

S: Work in rib pattern to the last 2 sts, kfb, p1. **55 sts.**

L: Work in rib pattern to the last 3 sts, k2tog, k1. **77 sts.**

XL: Work in rib pattern to the last 2 sts, kfb, p1. **88 sts.**

Leg

Some of you will be switching to bigger needles to knit the body of your sock, and some of you won't. Sizes **S** and **M,** switch to US size 2 (2.75 mm) needles. Sizes **L** and **XL**, cont working the body of your sock in US size 1 (2.25 mm) needles. The smaller sizes are using stitch counts close to the norm; however the larger sizes are working with more sts, so we don't need the bigger needles since those extra sts give us the extra fabric we need.

Work 2 rnds of Stockinette (knit every stitch), then work rnds 1–12 of the Forget-Me-Not Chart.

Note: If you plan on knitting your Leg longer, cont working all 15 rnds of the chart until your Leg is the desired length. Stop to place the marker for your Heel after working rnd 12.

Placing the Marker for the Afterthought Heel

You should be on rnd 13 of the chart. K**41 (50, 58, 66)** sts and clip a clasp marker onto that last st you just knit. Then just keep knitting to the end of the rnd. You have now marked where your Afterthought Heel will eventually go.

Foot

Repeat all 15 rnds of the chart (you should be starting on rnd 14) until your Foot reaches your desired length. The Craft Yarn Council has issued the following guidelines for the Foot of a sock, measured from the back of the Heel to the end of the Toe.

(All sizes are US.)
Women's shoe sizes 4–6.5: 8–9" (20.25–23 cm)
Women's shoe sizes 7–9.5: 9¼–10" (23.5–25.5 cm)
Women's shoe sizes 10–12.5: 10¼–11" (26–28 cm)
Men's shoe sizes 6–8.5: 9¼–10" (23.5–25.5 cm)
Men's shoe sizes 9–11.5: 10¼–11" (26–28 cm)
Men's shoe sizes 12–14: 11¼–12" (28.5–30.5 cm)

When working an Afterthought Heel, you need to take into account both your Heel length and your Toe length (they will be the same).

S: 1½" (4 cm)
M: 1½" (4 cm)
L: 1½" (4 cm)
XL: 1¾" (4 cm)

Now, take your desired Foot length, from the back of the Heel to the end of the Toe, and subtract both your Heel and Toe measurements. For example, my desired Foot length is 9" (23 cm). I subtract my Toe (1½" [4 cm]), and my Heel (1½" [4 cm]), and that leaves me with 6" (15 cm) I need to knit before starting my Toe decreases.

Setup for Toe Decreases

Break CC1 and CC2. Our stitch counts are for an 11-st chart. We'll need a setup round to get our counts right for the Toe Decreases. Make sure to work the setup rnd that corresponds with your size.

Setup Rnd 1
S: K1, ssk, k22, k2tog, k2, ssk, k24. **52 sts.**
M: K1, ssk, k31, ssk, k31. **64 sts.**
L: K1, ssk, k33, k2tog, k2, ssk, k35. **74 sts.**
XL: No setup rnd needed. Go straight to Toe Decreases below.

Toe Decreases

Using MC, knit 1 rnd even in Stockinette, then begin the following decrease pattern to shape your Toe:

Rnd 1: K1, ssk, k**20 (26, 31, 38)** sts, k2tog, k1, pm, k1, ssk, k**20 (26, 31, 38)** sts, k2tog, k1.

Rnd 2: Knit.

Rnd 3: K1, ssk, knit to 3 sts before next marker, k2tog, k1, sl m, k1, ssk, knit around to 3 sts before end of rnd, k2tog, k1.

Repeat rnds 2 and 3 until **24 (28, 34, 40)** sts remain.

Use Kitchener Stitch to close up your Toe.

Knitting the Afterthought Heel

You should have a long tube with a Cuff at one end and a Toe at the other end. Go to the point in your tube where you placed the clasp marker. Make sure your tube is pressed flat. You should have half your sts facing up at you and the other half of your sts facing down. Your Toe should look like a wedge, with the decrease lines on the sides of the wedge.

Identify the line of sts directly below the clasp marker. Select the first st at the edge of your tube. With US size 1 (2.25 mm) needles, insert the needle into the right leg of that first st. Next, insert the needle into the right leg of the second st and then into the right leg of the third st. Cont inserting your needle into the right leg of every st until you have picked up **28 (32, 36, 40)** sts. Next, repeat that process for the line of sts on the other side of your marked st. You should have **56 (64, 72, 80)** sts total divided evenly on your needles.

Remove the marker and tease that st up with your tapestry needle. Snip that st, being very careful not to snip anything else! Use your tapestry needle to tease out the yarn you've snipped from the sts. Start in the middle and go to the end on either side of your snipped st.

You now have a gaping hole in your sock tube and live Heel sts on the needles, ready to be worked. You also have a strand of yarn dangling on each side of the hole. Those will come in handy later when you weave in your ends. I use them to close gaps at the corners of the Heel.

Join in MC and knit 2 rnds even in Stockinette, then begin decreasing for your Heel:

Rnd 1: K1, ssk, k**22 (26, 30, 34)** sts, k2tog, k1, pm, k1, ssk, k**22 (26, 30, 34)**, k2tog, k1.

Rnd 2: Knit.

Rnd 3: K1, ssk, knit to 3 sts before next marker, k2tog, k1, sl m, k1, ssk, knit around to 3 sts before end of rnd, k2tog, k1.

Repeat rnds 2 and 3 until **24 (28, 32, 36)** sts remain.

Note: You can adjust the depth and fit of your Heel by working more or fewer decrease rnds. Try the sock on occasionally as you work your decreases to see how it's fitting. Stop your decreases when you can easily pinch the fabric closed.

Use Kitchener Stitch to close up your Heel.

Finishing

Weave in all your ends and block your socks.

Lobstah Socks

Maine just looks like this all the time.

The best thing about charming, historic New England towns is the bookstores!

In the summer of 2021 we sold our house, packed up our possessions, and drove for three exhausting days to the mythical state of Maine. We were headed (so we thought) for a new life where snow would fall, leaves would flame under a waning autumnal sun, and the ocean would always be right around the next bend, instead of a thousand miles away.

I am writing this from my spot on the couch in Tulsa, Oklahoma, so clearly our attempt to settle in a strange and foreign land did not shake out. It was an expensive failure on paper, but regret is not my way. Maine was not meant for me in that season of my life, but that magical summer we spent exploring her coastline, her deep, dark woods, and all the little ancient villages along the roads we traveled was life changing.

Is it a tad basic to design a pair of Lobstah Socks to commemorate my time in Maine? It's beyond basic, but I don't care. Lobsters are beautiful, marvelous creatures! They remind me of an otherworldly summer where I existed outside of the familiar and spent my days confronting one unknown after another. Also, they look sickeningly cute on a pair of socks, especially when paired with jaunty stripes, and that's reason enough to knit them.

DIFFICULTY LEVEL

Intermediate

SKILLS

Stranded knitting
Managing long floats
Heel flap and gusset
Striped knitting

MATERIALS

Yarn

Hedgehog Fibres Sock [90% superwash merino/10% nylon; 437 yards (400 m); 3½ ounces (100 g)]: 28 (42, 42) yards [26 (38, 38) m] in Silence (MC)

Knit Picks Stroll [75% fine superwash merino/25% nylon; 230 yards (210 m); 1¾ ounces (50 g)]: 18 (30, 30) yards [16 (27, 27) m] in Buoy (CC1)

Knit Picks Stroll: 2 (3, 3) yards [2 (3, 3) m] in Black (CC2)

Cascade Heritage [75% merino/25% nylon; 437 yards (400 m); 3½ ounces (100 g)]: 60 (93, 93) yards [55 (85, 85) m] in 5713 Placid Blue (CC3)

Cascade Heritage: 47 (78, 78) yards [43 (71, 71) m] in 5682 White (CC4)

Needles

US size 1 (2.25 mm)
US size 2 (2.75 mm)

Notions

Measuring tape, stitch markers (including a clasp marker), snips, tapestry needle

GAUGE

32 sts = 4" (10 cm), knit in colorwork pattern on US size 2 (2.75 mm) needles in the round and blocked

SIZES

S (M, L)

MEASUREMENTS

The numbers below refer to the circumference of the ball of the foot, not the measurements of the finished sock.

7 (8, 9)" [18 (20, 23) cm]

LOBSTAH CHART

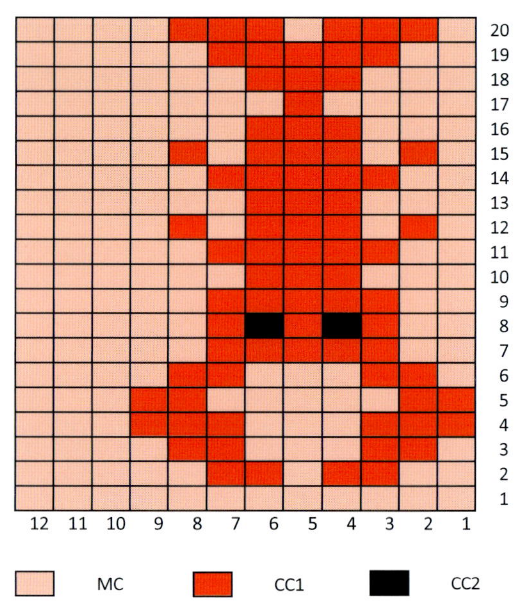

INSTRUCTIONS

Cuff

With MC and US size 1 (2.25 mm) needles, CO **60 (72, 72)** sts and join for working in the rnd, being careful not to twist your sts. Est 2×1 rib pattern: [k2, p1] to end.

Cont working est rib pattern until Cuff measures 1" (2.5 cm), or your desired length.

Leg

Sizes **S** and **L**, switch to US size 2 (2.75 mm) needles. Size **M**, cont knitting with US size 1 (2.25 mm) needles.

Work 2 rnds even in Stockinette, then work all 20 rnds of the Lobstah Chart *once.*

Break CC colors and work 4 rnds in Stockinette in MC.

Sizes **S** and **L**, switch back to US size 1 (2.25 mm) needles.

Break MC and begin working the stripe pattern in Stockinette as follows: 4 rnds CC4, 4 rnds CC3. *On the FIRST* rnd *ONLY* of the stripe pattern, Size **S** *ONLY*, work the following decreases:

K1, ssk, k25, k2tog, k2, ssk, knit around to 3 sts before the end of rnd, k2tog, k1. **56 sts.**

Cont working the stripe pattern until Leg, including Cuff, measures 4.5" (11 cm), or your desired length. End *after* working the last rnd of a CC4 stripe.

Heel Flap

With CC3, knit across the first **28 (36, 36)** sts, then begin working your Heel Flap back and forth across the remaining **28 (36, 36)** sts as follows:

Row 1 (RS): K2, [slip 1, k1] to end. Turn work.

Row 2 (WS): Slip 1 wyif, purl to end. Turn work.

Row 3: [Slip 1, k1] to end. Turn work.

Repeat rows 2 and 3 until Heel Flap measures **2 (2, 2¼)" [5 (5, 6) cm]**. End *after* you have worked row 3.

Heel Turn

Row 1 (WS): Slip 1 wyif, p**14 (18, 18)**, p2tog, p1, turn.

Row 2 (RS): Slip 1, k3, ssk, k1, turn.

Row 3: Slip 1 wyif, p4, p2tog, p1, turn.

Row 4: Slip 1, k5, ssk, k1, turn.

You have now established the following pattern for your Heel Turn: Slip 1, knit or purl to 1 st before the gap created by turning on the previous row, ssk or p2tog, k1 or p1, turn. Cont in this pattern until all your Heel sts have been worked, ending on a RS row. You should now have **16 (20, 20)** Heel sts.

Gusset

With the right side of your work facing, pick up and knit **12 (16, 16)** sts along the left side of your Heel Flap.

Next, work across the **28 (36, 36)** sts that we've left undisturbed on our needles while working our Heel Flap. Pm, and pick up **12 (16, 16)** sts on the right side of the Heel Flap. Knit across the Heel sts, then knit down the first set of new sts you picked up on the left side. You've reached the end of the rnd, and all your sts have now been picked up. You should now have **68 (88, 88)** sts on your needles.

Gusset Decreases

Rnd 1: Work in est stripe pattern across **28 (36, 36)** sts, sl m, k1, ssk, knit around to 3 sts before the end of rnd, k2tog, k1.

Rnd 2: Work even with no decreases.

Repeat these 2 rnds until you have **56 (64, 72)** sts on your needles.

Foot

Cont working in Stockinette in est stripe pattern until your Foot reaches just to the tip of your pinky toe. If you can't easily try on your socks as you knit (working on double-pointed needles or tiny circulars can make this challenging), or if you are knitting gift socks for some lucky recipient, the Craft Yarn Council has issued the following length guidelines for the Foot of a sock, measured from the back of the Heel to the end of the Toe.

(All sizes are US.)

Women's shoe sizes 4–6.5: 8–9" (20.25–23 cm)
Women's shoe sizes 7–9.5: 9¼–10" (23.5–25.5 cm)
Women's shoe sizes 10–12.5: 10¼–11" (26–28 cm)
Men's shoe sizes 6–8.5: 9¼–10" (23.5–25.5 cm)
Men's shoe sizes 9–11.5: 10¼–11" (26–28 cm)
Men's shoe sizes 12–14: 11¼–12" (28.5–30.5 cm)

When working a Heel Flap and Gusset, you need to take into account your Toe length.

S: 1½" (4 cm)
M: 1½" (4 cm)
L: 1½" (4 cm)

Now, take your desired Foot length, from the back of the Heel to the end of the Toe, and subtract your Toe measurement. For example, my desired Foot length is 9" (23 cm). I subtract my Toe (1½" [4 cm]) and that leaves me with 7½" (19 cm) I need to knit before starting my Toe decreases. Measure starting at the back of the Heel.

Toe

Begin the following decrease pattern for your Toes:

Rnd 1: K1, ssk, k**22 (26, 30)** sts, k2tog, k1, pm, k1, ssk, k**22 (26, 30)** sts, k2tog, k1.

Rnd 2: Knit.

Rnd 3: K1, ssk, knit to 3 sts before next marker, k2tog, k1, sl m, k1, ssk, knit around to 3 sts before end of rnd, k2tog, k1.

Repeat rnds 2 and 3 until **24 (28, 32)** sts remain.

Use Kitchener Stitch to close up your Toe.

Finishing

Weave in all your ends and block your socks.

Sheep Festival Socks

The arrival of September brings with it the promise of the state fair. Rides are hastily assembled in the late summer heat, games are rigged under the cover of darkness, and all manner of foods are fried and shoved onto sticks.

One can stroll leisurely, ogling fellow fair-goers while gnawing happily on a pickle that's been coated in enough batter and grease to oil a car engine. There are blue-ribbon pies to be inspected, sleek fattened pigs to be trotted out, and long lines to complain about.

I go to the fair for all those things, but the real draw for me is the sheep. Almost all knitters share an affinity with Animalia *Ovis*, those placid creatures that grow our favorite thing—yarn. From a distance, a flock of sheep roaming a hillside looks like a Renaissance painting. Pastoral. Calming. Beatific. Up close, however, sheep are kind of gross. Cute, yes, but even the most ardent sheep fan can't deny that they are best viewed from the front, rather than behind.

An interesting fact about sheep is that they can remember the faces of dozens of other sheep for two years. I'm desperately curious to know how scientists figured *that* out. Were they showing the sheep flash cards with sheep portraits on them? It's nice to think that a sheep who might have gotten lost, and then found his way home after many months picking his way through the wild, would be recognized by his flock when he came straggling back, thorns in his wool, emotional trauma from his trials and tribulations still fresh.

Me with my beloved Grassy (our nickname for Grandma) at the Oklahoma State Fair, about to murder a corn dog

The Sheep Festival Socks were designed with the community of the flock in mind. I like thinking of a merry band of sheep, their moods festive as they graze on a cool morning, greeting one another and partying it up in the pasture. Knit with an eight-stitch repeat, these socks are easy to knit, even for beginners. Have fun with your colors—knit white or black sheep, or neon green sheep!

DIFFICULTY LEVEL

Advanced beginner

SKILLS

Stranded knitting
Afterthought heel

MATERIALS

Yarn

Coates & Co. Cottage Sock [75% superwash merino/25% nylon; 437 yards (400 m); 3½ ounces (100 g)]: 109 (131, 158, 179) yards [100 (120, 144, 164) m] in Color No. 05 Coral (MC)

Cascade Heritage [75% merino/25% nylon; 437 yards (400 m); 3½ ounces (100 g)]: 42 (56, 68, 79) yards [38 (51, 62, 72) m] in 5682 White (CC1)

Cascade Heritage: 19 (27, 36, 43) yards [17 (25, 33, 39) m] in 5672 Real Black (CC2)

Needles

US size 1 (2.25 mm)
US size 2 (2.75 mm)

Notions

Measuring tape, stitch markers (including a clasp marker), snips, tapestry needle

GAUGE

32 sts = 4" (10 cm), knit in colorwork pattern on US size 2 (2.75 mm) needles in the round and blocked

SIZES

S (M, L, XL)

MEASUREMENTS

The numbers below refer to the circumference of the ball of the foot, not the measurements of the finished sock.

7 (8, 9, 10)" [18 (20, 23, 25) cm]

SHEEP CHART

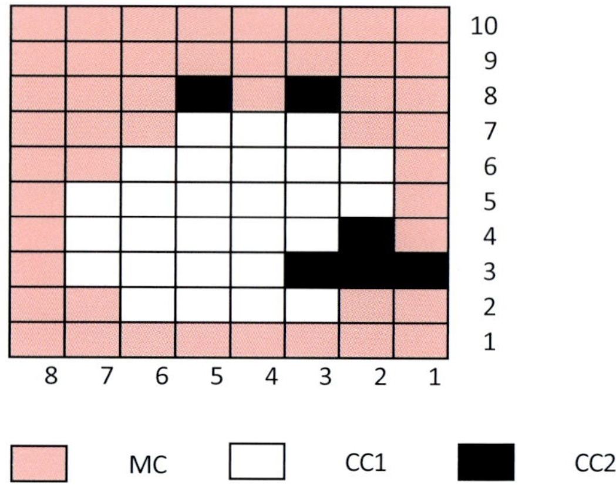

INSTRUCTIONS

Cuff

With US size 1 (2.25 mm) needles and MC, CO **57 (63, 72, 81)** sts and join for working in the rnd, being careful not to twist your sts. Est 2×1 ribbing: [k2, p1] to end.

Cont working the ribbing until your Cuff measures ¾" (2 cm), or your desired length.

Leg

Switch to US size 2 (2.75 mm) needles and work 1 rnd even in Stockinette, making the following inc or dec according to your size:

S: Work to last 3 sts, k2tog, k1. **56 sts.**
M: Work to last 2 sts, kfb, k1. **64 sts.**
L: No inc or dec. **72 sts.**
XL: Work to last 3 sts, k2tog, k1. **80 sts.**

Work 2 more rnds even in Stockinette, then work rnds 1–9 of the Sheep Chart once before stopping to place your marker for the Afterthought Heel.

Note: If you'd like a longer Leg, simply repeat all 10 rnds of the chart until your Leg, including the Cuff, reaches your desired length. Stop to place your Afterthought Heel marker after you have completed rnd 9.

Placing the Marker for the Afterthought Heel

You should be on rnd 10 of the chart. To place your marker, simply knit **42 (48, 54, 60)** sts, and clip a clasp marker onto that last st you just knit. Then just keep knitting to the end of the rnd. You have now marked where your Afterthought Heel will eventually go, and you should now be ready to work rnd 1 of the chart.

Foot

Cont repeating all 10 rnds of the Sheep Chart until your Foot reaches the desired length. The Craft Yarn Council has issued the following guidelines for the Foot of a sock, measured from the back of the Heel to the end of the Toe.

(All sizes are US.)
Women's shoe sizes 4–6.5: 8–9" (20.25–23 cm)
Women's shoe sizes 7–9.5: 9¼–10" (23.5–25.5 cm)
Women's shoe sizes 10–12.5: 10¼–11" (26–28 cm)
Men's shoe sizes 6–8.5: 9¼–10" (23.5–25.5 cm)
Men's shoe sizes 9–11.5: 10¼–11" (26–28 cm)
Men's shoe sizes 12–14: 11¼–12" (28.5–30.5 cm)

When working an Afterthought Heel, you need to take into account both your Heel length and your Toe length (they will be the same).

S: 1½" (4 cm)
M: 1½" (4 cm)
L: 1½" (4 cm)
XL: 1¾" (4 cm)

Now, take your desired Foot length, from the back of the Heel to the end of the Toe, and subtract both your Heel and Toe measurements. For example, my desired Foot length is 9" (23 cm). I subtract my Toe (1½" [4 cm]) and my Heel (1½" [4 cm]) and that leaves me with 6" (15 cm) I need to knit before starting my Toe decreases.

Toe

Break CC colors and switch back to US size 1 (2.25 mm) needles. Using MC, knit 1 rnd even in Stockinette, then begin the following decrease pattern to shape your Toe:

Rnd 1: K1, ssk, k**22 (26, 30, 34)** sts, k2tog, k1, pm, k1, ssk, k**22 (26, 30, 34)** sts, k2tog, k1.

Rnd 2: Knit.

Rnd 3: K1, ssk, knit to 3 sts before next marker, k2tog, k1, sl m, k1, ssk, knit around to 3 sts before end of rnd, k2tog, k1.

Repeat rnds 2 and 3 until **24 (28, 32, 36)** sts remain.

Use Kitchener Stitch to close up your Toe.

Knitting the Afterthought Heel

You should have a long tube with a Cuff at one end and a Toe at the other end. Go to the point in your tube where you placed the clasp marker. Make sure your tube is pressed flat. You should have half your sts facing up at you and the other half of your sts facing down. Your Toe should look like a wedge, with the decrease lines on the sides of the wedge.

Identify the line of sts directly below the clasp marker. Select the first st at the edge of your tube. With US size 1 (2.25 mm) needles, insert the needle into the right leg of that first st. Next, insert the needle into the right leg of the second st, and then into the right leg of the third st. Cont inserting your needle into the right leg of every st until you have picked up **28 (32, 36, 40)** sts. Next, repeat that process for the line of sts on the other side of your waste yarn. You should have **56 (64, 72, 80)** sts total divided evenly on your needles.

Remove the marker and tease that st up with your tapestry needle. Snip that st, being very careful not to snip anything else! Use your tapestry needle to tease out the yarn you've snipped from the sts. Start in the middle and go to the end on either side of your snipped st.

You now have a gaping hole in your sock tube and live Heel sts on the needles, ready to be worked. You also have a strand of yarn dangling on each side of the hole. Those will come in handy later when you weave in your ends. I use them to close gaps at the corners of the Heel.

You will work your Afterthought Heel the same as your Toe. Join in your yarn. Sizes **Kid and L**, work 3 rnds even in Stockinette, then move on to the Heel Decreases below.

Sizes **S, M, XL** ONLY, work the following setup rnd prior to working the Heel:

S: K1, ssk, k25, k2tog, knit around to end. 52 sts.

M: K1, ssk, k31, k2tog, knit around to end. 64 sts.

XL: K1, ssk, k37, k2tog, knit around to end. 76 sts.

Work 2 more rnds even in Stockinette, then begin working the Heel Decreases.

Join in MC and knit 2 rnds even in Stockinette, then begin the following decrease pattern for your Heel:

Rnd 1: K1, ssk, k**22 (26, 30, 34)**, k2tog, k1, pm, k1, ssk, k**22 (26, 30, 34)**, k2tog, k1.

Rnd 2: Knit.

Rnd 3: K1, ssk, knit to 3 sts before next marker, k2tog, k1, sl m, k1, ssk, knit around to 3 sts before end of rnd, k2tog, k1.

Repeat rnds 2 and 3 until **24 (28, 32, 36)** sts remain.

Note: You can adjust the depth and fit of your Heel by working more or fewer decrease rnds. Try the sock on occasionally as you work your decreases to see how it's fitting. Stop your decreases when you can easily pinch the fabric closed.

Use Kitchener Stitch to close up your Heel.

Finishing

Weave in all your ends and block your socks.

Drew's Socks

That's my nephew Drew in the middle between my teens.

My nephew Drew's obsession with all things fungal inspired these socks. You should see the way his face lights up when he gets ripping on spore disbursement. He's a scientist at heart, always deeply curious about the natural world. (He once fermented his own wine under the sink in his bathroom. There was an explosion, and my brother, unaware that Drew had been amateur winemaking, was surprised, but not *that* surprised, to find decimated grape particles all over the bathroom.)

Although all mushrooms are intricate, beautiful organisms, no mushroom is more photographed or drawn than the toxic *Amanita muscaria*, those little red-capped fellows with the jaunty white dots. They're insanely cute, and easily the most recognizable fungus. They're called toadstools for goodness' sake—how can we not put them in illustrated fairy tale books?

They're irresistible to knit as well. Mushroom socks were at the top of my list of whimsical things to design for this book. I kept my knit *Amanita* to the top of the sock, pairing them with a sweet texture stitch on a tweed yarn to create socks straight out of a magic fable.

DIFFICULTY LEVEL

Intermediate

SKILLS

Stranded knitting

Managing long floats

Heel flap and gusset

MATERIALS

Yarn

Little Lionhead Knits Fingering Weight BFL Tweed [85% superwash Bluefaced Leicester/ 15% Donegal Nep; 438 yards (400 m); 3½ ounces (100 g)]: 101 (128, 147, 165) yards [92 (117, 134, 151) m] in Mystery (MC)

La Bien Aimée Super Sock [75% superwash merino/25% nylon; 465 yards (425 m); 3½ ounces (100 g)]: 38 (44, 52, 59) yards [35 (40, 48, 54) m] in Jonna (CC1)

Knit Picks Stroll [75% fine superwash merino/25% nylon; 231 yards (211 m); 1¾ ounces (50 g)]: 16 (21, 27, 32) yards [15 (19, 25, 29) m] in Buoy (CC2)

Knit Picks Stroll: 13 (18, 24, 28) yards [12 (16, 22, 26) m] in White (CC3)

Needles

US size 1 (2.25 mm)

US size 2 (2.75 mm)

Notions

Measuring tape, stitch markers (including a clasp marker), snips, tapestry needle

GAUGE

32 sts = 4" (10 cm), knit in colorwork pattern on US size 2 (2.75 mm) needles in the round and blocked

SIZES

S (M, L, XL)

MEASUREMENTS

The numbers below refer to the circumference of the ball of the foot, not the measurements of the finished sock.

7 (8, 9, 10)" [18 (20, 23, 25) cm]

MUSHROOM CHART

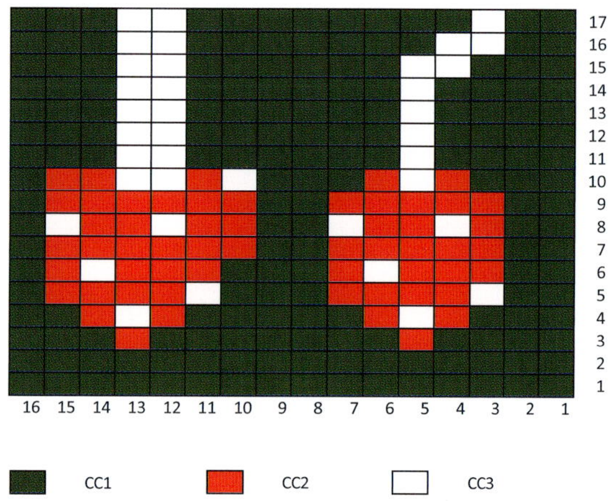

INSTRUCTIONS

Cuff

Note: Because of the stitch counts for this pattern, some of you will be working with more stitches, and some of you will be working with bigger needles to get the amount of fabric stretch you need on the colorwork portion. Pay special attention to the instructions for your size to ensure you get the proper fit.

With CC1 and US size 1 (2.25 mm) needles, CO **63 (63, 81, 81)** sts and join for working in the rnd, being careful not to twist your sts. Est 2×1 ribbing pattern: [k2, p1] to end.

Cont working ribbing pattern until Cuff measures 1" (2.5 cm) or your desired length.

Sizes **M** and **XL**, switch to US size 2 (2.75 mm) needles. Sizes **S** and **L**, cont working with US size 1 (2.25 mm) needles. Both sizes work 1 rnd even in Stockinette, making the following inc or dec according to your size:

S/M: Work to last 2 sts, kfb, k1. **64 sts.**
L/XL: Work to last 3 sts, k2tog, k1. **80 sts.**

Work all 17 rnds of the Mushroom Chart *once*. Break CC2 and CC3, then work 4 rnds even in CC1.

Break CC1 and switch back to US size 1 (2.25 mm) needles (sizes **M** and **XL**). Join in MC and knit 1 rnd even, then begin the following texture pattern:

Rnd 1: [K1, p1] to end.
Rnd 2: Knit.

Cont repeating both rnds of the texture pattern until Leg, including Cuff, measures 4" (10 cm).

Heel Flap

Knit across the first **32 (32, 40, 40)** sts, then begin working your Heel Flap back and forth across the remaining **32 (32, 40, 40)** sts as follows:

Row 1 (RS): K2, [slip 1, k1] to end. Turn work.

Row 2 (WS): Slip 1 wyif, purl to end. Turn work.

Row 3: [Slip 1, k1] to end. Turn work.

Repeat rows 2 and 3 until Heel Flap measures **2 (2, 2¼, 2½)" [5 (5, 6, 6.5) cm]**. End *after* you have worked row 3.

Heel Turn

Row 1 (WS): Slip 1 wyif, p**16 (16, 20, 20)**, p2tog, p1, turn.

Row 2 (RS): Slip 1, k3, ssk, k1, turn.

Row 3: Slip 1 wyif, p4, p2tog, p1, turn.

Row 4: Slip 1, k5, ssk, k1, turn.

You have now established the following pattern for your Heel Turn: Slip 1, knit or purl to 1 st before the gap created by turning on the previous row, ssk or p2tog, k1 or p1, turn. Cont in this pattern until all your Heel sts have been worked, ending on a RS row. You should now have **18 (18, 22, 22)** Heel sts.

Gusset

With the right side of your work facing, pick up and knit **12 (14, 16, 18)** sts along the left side of your Heel Flap.

Next, work in est texture pattern across the **32 (32, 40, 40)** sts that we've left undisturbed on our needles while working our Heel Flap. Pm, and pick up **12 (14, 16, 18)** sts on the right side of the Heel Flap. Knit across the Heel sts, then knit down the first set of new sts you picked up on the left side. You've reached the end of the rnd, and all your sts have now been picked up.

Gusset Decreases

Rnd 1: Work in texture pattern across **32 (32, 40, 40)** sts, sl m, k1, ssk, knit around to 3 sts before the end of rnd, k2tog, k1.

Rnd 2: Work even with no decreases.

Repeat these 2 rnds until you have **64 (64, 80, 80)** sts on your needles.

Foot

Cont working texture pattern across the first **32 (32, 40, 40)** sts and in Stockinette across the remaining sts until your Foot reaches just to the tip of your pinky toe. If you can't easily try on your socks as you knit (working on double-pointed needles or tiny circulars can make this challenging), or if you are knitting gift socks for some lucky recipient, the Craft Yarn Council has issued the following length guidelines for the Foot of a sock, measured from the back of the Heel to the end of the Toe.

(All sizes are US.)

Women's shoe sizes 4–6.5: 8–9" (20.25–23 cm)
Women's shoe sizes 7–9.5: 9¼–10" (23.5–25.5 cm)
Women's shoe sizes 10–12.5: 10¼–11" (26–28 cm)
Men's shoe sizes 6–8.5: 9¼–10" (23.5–25.5 cm)
Men's shoe sizes 9–11.5: 10¼–11" (26–28 cm)
Men's shoe sizes 12–14: 11¼–12" (28.5–30.5 cm)

When working a Heel Flap and Gusset, you need to take into account your Toe length.

S: 1½" (4 cm)
M: 1½" (4 cm)
L: 1½" (4 cm)
XL: 1¾" (4 cm)

Now, take your desired Foot length, from the back of the Heel to the end of the Toe, and subtract your Toe measurements. For example, my desired Foot length is 9" (23 cm). I subtract my Toe (1½" [4 cm]) and that leaves me with 7½" (19 cm) I need to knit before starting my Toe decreases. Measure starting at the back of the Heel.

Toe

Begin the following decrease pattern for your Toes:

Rnd 1: K1, ssk, k**26 (26, 34, 34)** sts, k2tog, k1, pm, k1, ssk, k**26 (26, 34, 34)** sts, k2tog, k1.

Rnd 2: Knit.

Rnd 3: K1, ssk, knit to 3 sts before next marker, k2tog, k1, sl m, k1, ssk, knit around to 3 sts before end of rnd, k2tog, k1.

Repeat rnds 2 and 3 until **28 (28, 32, 32)** sts remain.

Use Kitchener Stitch to close up your Toe.

Finishing

Weave in all your ends and block your socks.

Bumblebee Socks

Did you know that blueberry farmers keep hives of bees around to help pollinate their fields? And sometimes those hives just take off and regroup on the side of someone's house? I didn't know that either until my summer in Maine. We were looking at a house that was for sale in a postcard-perfect village far up the coast. As we were walking around the home's perimeter, admiring all the lovely historical details on the exterior, I looked up and about peed my pants. Congregating on half of the second story was a massive, humming, ominous beard of bees. The real estate agent was like, "Aw, Mack's bees are loose again," like it was just any normal Tuesday in Maine's blueberry corridor.

As terrifying as it was to be mere feet from a massive, teeming colony of Maine bees, it was also wicked awesome. The pollinators of our world, responsible for Mack's blueberry crop apparently, were undulating in mysterious ways known only to them, and I was mesmerized by their coordinated movements. It was only our third day in Maine, and already astonishing things were happening.

We didn't end up buying that house (or any other house in Maine), but the swarming bees are a core memory for me, and thus knitting bee socks was a necessity. I paired my little colony with an appropriately royal purple background, since bee symbology has been synonymous with royalty throughout history. My daughter has already warned me she plans to steal these socks, so they're teen-approved, too.

DIFFICULTY LEVEL

Intermediate

SKILLS

Stranded knitting
Managing long floats
Afterthought heel

MATERIALS

Yarn

I hand-dyed the purple yarn in my sample socks myself. I've included a comparable color below.

Hedgehog Fibres Sock [90% superwash merino/10% nylon; 437 yards (400 m); 3½ ounces (100 g)]: 92, (109, 131, 156) yards [84 (100, 120, 143) m] in Hush (MC)

Knit Picks Stroll [75% fine superwash merino wool/25% nylon; 230 yards (211 m); 1¾ ounces (50 g)]: 23 (31, 40, 49) yards [21 (28, 37, 45) m] in Black (CC1)

Knit Picks Stroll: 17 (26, 35, 44) yards [16 (24, 32, 40) m] in Dandelion (CC2)

Knit Picks Stroll: 13 (20, 27, 34) yards [12 (18, 25, 31) m] in White (CC3)

Needles

US size 1 (2.25 mm)

US size 2 (2.75 mm)

Notions

Measuring tape, stitch markers (including a clasp marker), snips, tapestry needle

GAUGE

32 sts = 4" (10 cm), knit in colorwork pattern on US size 2 (2.75 mm) needles in the round and blocked

SIZES

S (M, L, XL)

MEASUREMENTS

The numbers below refer to the circumference of the ball of the foot, not the measurements of the finished sock.

7 (8, 9, 10)" [18 (20, 23, 25) cm]

BUMBLEBEE CHART

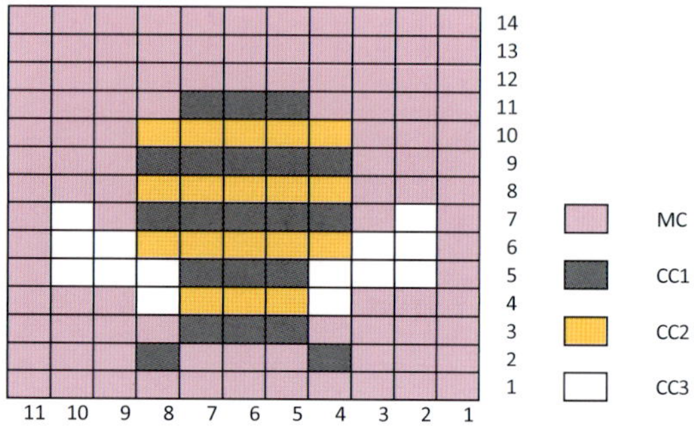

INSTRUCTIONS

Cuff

With MC and US size 1 (2.25 mm) needles, CO **54 (66, 78, 87)** sts and join for working in the rnd, being careful not to twist your sts. Est 2×1 ribbing: [k2, p1] to end.

Cont working the ribbing until your Cuff measures ¾" (2 cm), or your desired length. On the last rnd of the ribbing, we need to get our stitch count to the right amount for the chart. If you are working the size **M**, you already have the right number and can move on to the Leg instructions. The rest of you, make the following increase or decrease according to your size:

S: Work in rib pattern to the last 2 sts, kfb, p1. **55 sts.**

L: Work in rib pattern to the last 3 sts, k2tog, k1. **77 sts.**

XL: Work in rib pattern to the last 2 sts, kfb, p1. **88 sts.**

Leg

Some of you will be switching to bigger needles to knit the body of your sock, and some of you won't. Sizes **S** and **M**, switch to US size 2 (2.75 mm) needles. Sizes **L** and **XL**, cont working the body of your sock in US size 1 (2.25 mm) needles. The smaller sizes are using stitch counts close to the norm; however, the larger sizes are working with more sts, so we don't need the bigger needles since those extra sts give us the extra fabric we need.

Work 2 rnds of Stockinette (knit every stitch), then work rnds 1–12 of the Bumblebee Chart.

Note: If you plan on knitting your Leg longer, cont working all 14 rnds of the chart until your Leg is the desired length. Stop to place the marker for your Heel after working rnd 12.

Placing the Marker for the Afterthought Heel

You should be on rnd 13 of the chart. K**41 (50, 58, 66)** sts and clip a clasp marker onto that last st you just knit. Then just keep knitting to the end of the rnd. You have now marked where your Afterthought Heel will eventually go.

Foot

Repeat all 14 rnds of the chart (you should be starting on rnd 14) until your Foot reaches your desired length. The Craft Yarn Council has issued the following guidelines for the Foot of a sock, measured from the back of the Heel to the end of the Toe.

(All sizes are US.)
Women's shoe sizes 4–6.5: 8–9" (20.25–23 cm)
Women's shoe sizes 7–9.5: 9¼–10" (23.5–25.5 cm)
Women's shoe sizes 10–12.5: 10¼–11" (26–28 cm)
Men's shoe sizes 6–8.5: 9¼–10" (23.5–25.5 cm)
Men's shoe sizes 9–11.5: 10¼–11" (26–28 cm)
Men's shoe sizes 12–14: 11¼–12" (28.5–30.5 cm)

When working an Afterthought Heel, you need to take into account both your Heel length and your Toe length (they will be the same).

S: 1½" (4 cm)
M: 1½" (4 cm)
L: 1½" (4 cm)
XL: 1¾" (4 cm)

Now take your desired Foot length, from the back of the Heel to the end of the Toe, and subtract both your Heel and Toe measurements. For example, my desired Foot length is 9" (23 cm). I subtract my Toe (1½" [4 cm]) and my Heel (1½" [4 cm]) and that leaves me with 6" (15 cm) I need to knit before starting my Toe Decreases.

Setup for Toe Decreases

Break CC1 and CC2. Our stitch counts are for an 11-st colorwork chart. We'll need to do a setup round to get our counts right for the Toe Decreases. Make sure to work the setup rnd that corresponds with your size.

Setup Rnd 1
S: K1, ssk, k22, k2tog, k2, ssk, k24. **52 sts.**

M: K1, ssk, k31, ssk, k31. **64 sts.**

L: K1, ssk, k33, k2tog, k2, ssk, k35. **74 sts.**

XL: No setup rnd needed. Go straight to Toe Decreases below.

Toe Decreases

Using MC, knit 1 rnd even in Stockinette, then begin decreasing to shape your Toe:

Rnd 1: K1, ssk, k**20 (26, 31, 38)** sts, k2tog, k1, pm, k1, ssk, k**20 (26, 31, 38)** sts, k2tog, k1.

Rnd 2: Knit.

Rnd 3: K1, ssk, knit to 3 sts before next marker, k2tog, k1, sl m, k1, ssk, knit around to 3 sts before end of rnd, k2tog, k1.

Repeat rnds 2 and 3 until **24 (28, 34, 40)** sts remain.

Use Kitchener Stitch to close up your Toe.

Knitting the Afterthought Heel

You should have a long tube with a Cuff at one end and a Toe at the other end. Go to the point in your tube where you placed the clasp marker. Make sure your tube is pressed flat. You should have half your sts facing up at you and the other half of your sts facing down. Your Toe should look like a wedge, with the decrease lines on the sides of the wedge.

Identify the line of sts directly below the clasp marker. Select the first st at the edge of your tube. With US size 1 (2.25 mm) needles, insert the needle into the right leg of that first st. Next, insert the needle into the right leg of the second st, and then into the right leg of the third st. Cont inserting your needle into the right leg of every st until you have picked up **28 (32, 36, 40)** sts. Next, repeat that process for the line of sts on the other side of your marked st. You should have **56 (64, 72, 80)** sts total divided evenly on your needles.

Remove the marker and tease that st up with your tapestry needle. Snip that st, being very careful not to snip anything else! Use your tapestry needle to tease out the yarn you've snipped from the sts. Start in the middle and go to the end on either side of your snipped st.

You now have a gaping hole in your sock tube and live Heel sts on the needles, ready to be worked. You also have a strand of yarn dangling on each side of the hole. Those will come in handy later when you weave in your ends. I use them to close gaps at the corners of the Heel.

Join in MC and knit 2 rnds even in Stockinette, then begin the following decrease pattern for your Heel:

Rnd 1: K1, ssk, k**22 (26, 30, 34)** sts, k2tog, k1, pm, k1, ssk, k**22 (26, 30, 34)** sts, k2tog, k1.

Rnd 2: Knit.

Rnd 3: K1, ssk, knit to 3 sts before next marker, k2tog, k1, sl m, k1, ssk, knit around to 3 sts before end of rnd, k2tog, k1.

Repeat rnds 2 and 3 until **24 (28, 32, 36)** sts remain.

Note: You can adjust the depth and fit of your Heel by working more or fewer decrease rnds. Try the sock on occasionally as you work your decreases to see how it's fitting. Stop your decreases when you can easily pinch the fabric closed.

Use Kitchener Stitch to close up your Heel.

Finishing

Weave in all your ends and block your socks.

Chapter 5

SUMMER'S SIGNATURE SOCKS

Five years ago I shared a photo on Instagram that would change the trajectory of my life. It was only the beginning of a sock, just a cuff and a few inches of the leg, knit in a pink speckled yarn. I balanced it precariously in the palm of my hand, took a quick picture, and posted it, thinking it looked like a little sock cupcake.

That picture blew up, my obsession with sock knitting took off, and a few months later I was headed to the bank to open a business checking account (the banker, by the way, probably thought I was laundering money when I explained that my business involved designing sock knitting patterns and selling them to people).

I don't even know how many patterns I've designed at this point, and I'm too lazy to look it up. But I can emphatically say that each pattern I've ever released into the world has been designed to suit my own personal whims, wishes, and wants. I don't design socks that I think other people might like. I only design socks that I personally love, and I just hope other people will love them too.

The socks in this chapter are the ones I personally love the most. They are my absolute favorites, the ones that I'm most proud of, the ones that I'm, well, obsessed with. There is an abundance of bright color (obviously), and texture, and joy, and stripes (of course). They are my signature style of explosively happy socks, and I hope when you knit them, you *feel* as happy as I did designing them.

Two-Way Striped Socks

We're old friends by now, so you're probably aware of my enduring love for stripes. In my old house, we had twelve-foot-tall walls, and my danger-loving self wobbled around on a rickety ladder for days hand-painting stripes the length and breadth of my entryway. And then we sold that house like two months later, so I risked my life for nothing.

Houses come and go, but hand-knit socks can last a lifetime (with careful wear and darning at least). It's much more sensible to indulge one's stripe obsession from the safety of the couch. Because one set of stripes on a pair of socks is absurdly awesome, I figured two sets of stripes going in two different directions, knit in a bajillion different colors, could possibly bend the space-time continuum out of sheer cuteness. I didn't feel the fabric of time ripping after knitting these, but maybe it would if we all knit them?

The infamous striped entryway! Notice the stripes going two different directions?

I'm sure a few of you are looking at these socks in horror given the number of ends that will need to be dealt with. (I gave up on hating ends a long time ago and basically rewired my brain to love weaving them in—a necessary adjustment given my obsession with using all the colors at once.) There are two solutions to this problem: First, you could knit these socks in just two colors, and, frankly, that would rule. So graphic and eye-catching! You can also follow my tips on page 27 for knitting stripes. I show you how to weave your ends in as you go, and that will get rid of most of them on this pair.

DIFFICULTY LEVEL

Advanced beginner

SKILLS

Stranded colorwork
Heel flap and gusset
Striped knitting

MATERIALS

Yarn

Lang Jawoll [75% virgin superwash wool/ 25% nylon; 230 yards (210 m); 1¾ ounces (50 g)]: 38 (47, 59, 68) yards [35 (43, 54, 62) m] in 23 Cloud Heather (MC)

I used little odds-and-ends scraps for these socks. They're a perfect stash buster. You'll need an assortment of fingering weight sock yarns in colors you love, to total the following yardage: 177 (201, 229, 246) yards [162 (184, 209, 225) m].

Needles

US size 1 (2.25 mm)
US size 2 (2.75 mm)

Notions

Measuring tape, stitch markers (including a clasp marker), snips, tapestry needle

GAUGE

32 sts = 4" (10 cm), knit in colorwork pattern on US size 2 (2.75 mm) needles in the round and blocked

SIZES

S (M, L, XL)

MEASUREMENTS

The numbers below refer to the circumference of the ball of the foot, not the measurements of the finished sock.

7 (8, 9, 10)" [18 (20, 23, 25) cm]

TWO-WAY STRIPED CHART

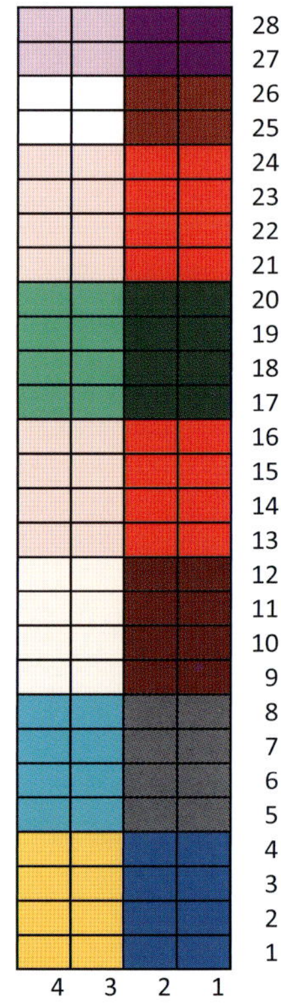

INSTRUCTIONS

Cuff

With MC and US size 1 (2.25 mm) needles, CO **57 (63, 72, 81)** sts and join for working in the rnd, being careful not to twist your sts. Est 2×1 ribbing: [k2, p1] to end.

Cont working the ribbing until your Cuff measures ¾" (2 cm), or your desired length. On the last rnd of the ribbing, we need to get our stitch count back to an even number. If you are working size **L**, you already have an even number and can move on to the Leg instructions. The rest of you, make the following increase or decrease according to your size:

S: Work in rib pattern to the last 3 sts, k2tog, p1. **56 sts.**

M: Work in rib pattern to the last 3 sts, kfb, k1, p1. **64 sts.**

XL: Work in rib pattern to the last 3 sts, k2tog, p1. **80 sts.**

Leg

Switch to US size 2 (2.75 mm) needles. Cut MC and join in your first color. Begin working the Two-Way Striped Chart. Work all 28 rnds of the chart *once*. Cut your last two colors and switch back to US size 1 (2.25 mm) needles.

From this point forward, you will be working simple stripes. Worried about weaving in all those ends? Refer to page 27 for some helpful tips on knitting your ends in as you go. You'll also find a tip on page 28 for avoiding a jog when you switch to a new color.

I worked my stripes in the same color order I worked my chart. You'll be working 4 rnds of each color. I worked 5 total colors before stopping for my Heel. The Leg (including Cuff) of my sample sock measures 5" (13 cm). If you'd like your Leg longer or shorter, simply work more or fewer stripes.

Heel Flap

With a new color, work across the first **28 (32, 36, 40)** sts. Join in MC (but don't cut your new color!), then begin working your Heel Flap back and forth with MC across the remaining **28 (32, 36, 40)** sts as follows:

Row 1 (RS): K2, [slip 1, k1] to end. Turn work.

Row 2 (WS): Slip 1 wyif, purl to end. Turn work.

Row 3: [Slip 1, k1] to end. Turn work.

Repeat rows 2 and 3 until Heel Flap measures **2 (2, 2¼, 2½)" [5 (5, 6, 6.5) cm]**. End *after* you have worked row 3.

Heel Turn

Row 1 (WS): Slip 1 wyif, p**14 (16, 18, 20)**, p2tog, p1, turn.

Row 2 (RS): Slip 1, k3, ssk, k1, turn.

Row 3: Slip 1 wyif, p4, p2tog, p1, turn.

Row 4: Slip 1, k5, ssk, k1, turn.

You have now established the following pattern for your Heel Turn: Slip 1, knit or purl to 1 st before the gap created by turning on the previous row, ssk or p2tog, k1 or p1, turn. Cont in this pattern until all your Heel sts have been worked, ending on a RS row. You should now have **16 (18, 20, 22)** Heel sts. Cut MC and resume working with the new color you started at the beginning of your Heel Flap journey.

Gusset

With the right side of your work facing, pick up and knit **12 (14, 16, 18)** sts along the left side of your Heel Flap. (You should be on rnd 2 of your current 4-rnd stripe.)

Next, work across the **28 (32, 36, 40)** sts that we've left undisturbed on our needles while working our Heel Flap. Pm, and pick up **12 (14, 16, 18)** sts on the right side of the Heel Flap. Knit across the Heel sts, then knit down the first set of new sts you picked up on the left side. You've reached the end of the rnd, and all your sts have now been picked up. You should now have **68 (78, 88, 98)** sts on your needles.

Gusset Decreases

Rnd 1: Work across **28 (32, 36, 40)** sts, sl m, k1, ssk, knit around to 3 sts before the end of rnd, k2tog, k1.

Rnd 2: Work even with no decreases.

Repeat these 2 rnds *while at the same time* maintaining your 4-rnd stripe pattern until you have **56 (64, 72, 80)** sts on your needles.

Foot

Cont working in the 4-rnd stripe pattern in Stockinette until your Foot reaches just to the tip of your pinky toe. If you can't easily try on your socks as you knit (working on double-pointed needles or tiny circulars can make this challenging), or if you are knitting gift socks for some lucky recipient, the Craft Yarn Council has issued the following length guidelines for the Foot of a sock, measured from the back of the Heel to the end of the Toe.

(All sizes are US.)

Women's shoe sizes 4–6.5: 8–9" (20.25–23 cm)
Women's shoe sizes 7–9.5: 9¼–10" (23.5–25.5 cm)
Women's shoe sizes 10–12.5: 10¼–11" (26–28 cm)
Men's shoe sizes 6–8.5: 9¼–10" (23.5–25.5 cm)
Men's shoe sizes 9–11.5: 10¼–11" (26–28 cm)
Men's shoe sizes 12–14: 11¼–12" (28.5–30.5 cm)

When working a Heel Flap and Gusset, you need to take into account your Toe length.

S: 1½" (4 cm)
M: 1½" (4 cm)
L: 1½" (4 cm)
XL: 1¾" (4 cm)

Now, take your desired Foot length, from the back of the Heel to the end of the Toe, and subtract your Toe measurement. For example, my desired Foot length is 9" (23 cm). I subtract my Toe (1½" [4 cm]) and that leaves me with 7½" (19 cm) I need to knit before starting my Toe decreases. Measure starting at the back of the Heel.

Toe

Cut your last stripe color and join in MC. Work 1 rnd even, then begin the following decrease pattern for your Toes:

Rnd 1: K1, ssk, k**22 (26, 30, 34)** sts, k2tog, k1, pm, k1, ssk, k**22 (26, 30, 34)** sts, k2tog, k1.

Rnd 2: Knit.

Rnd 3: K1, ssk, knit to 3 sts before next marker, k2tog, k1, sl m, k1, ssk, knit around to 3 sts before end of rnd, k2tog, k1.

Repeat rnds 2 and 3 until **24 (28, 32, 36)** sts remain.

Use Kitchener Stitch to close up your Toe.

Finishing

Weave in all your ends and block your socks.

Flight Socks

When I was in high school, I had a subscription to *Rolling Stone* magazine. It arrived every two weeks in the mail, having traveled halfway across the country to my little cow town in the middle of nowhere so that I could open its big pages and yearn, fiercely, to be anywhere else but Welch, Oklahoma. If I lived somewhere cool like Seattle, I could skulk around Sub Pop Records, hoping to catch sight of Mark Lanegan or Courtney Love. The only famous musician in my immediate area was Roy Clark, a country singer who had a ranch outside of town.

I was convinced that as soon as I graduated high school, I was going straight to the Pacific Northwest so I could write a novel and somehow become best friends with The Breeders (never mind that they were from Ohio). I would lay in the hayfield behind my house, watching the occasional plane pass overhead, imagining myself up in the sky heading toward adventure (and improbable friendships with musicians who were twenty years older than me).

What actually happened was that I stayed right here in Oklahoma. (Note to those of you reading this who are in your teens and twenties—get on that damn plane! Follow that band you love around the country! Have adventures RIGHT NOW!)

Me as a teen, oozing angst

The Flight Socks are my bittersweet requiem for all those planes I did not get on because I was too scared to do something radical on my own. Isn't it wild how the things we knit are a wearable record of our interior lives? These simple little triangle socks are so personal to me, and one of my favorite things I've ever knit, because when I look at them, I see teenage me lying out in that field with a *Rolling Stone*, dreaming of taking flight.

DIFFICULTY LEVEL

Advanced beginner

SKILLS

Stranded colorwork
Forethought heel

MATERIALS

Yarn

Lang Jawoll [75% virgin superwash wool/25% nylon; 230 yards (210 meters); 1¾ ounces (50 g)]: 48 (66, 83, 99) yards [44 (60, 76, 91) m] in 94 Pearl (MC)

Lang Jawoll: 59 (81, 97, 118) yards [54 (74, 89, 108) m] in 70 Charcoal (CC1)

Coates & Co. Cottage Sock [75% superwash merino/25% nylon; 437 yards (400 m); 3½ ounces (100 g)]: 14 (20, 26, 32) yards [13 (18, 24, 29) m] in Color No. 08 Bright Peach (CC2)

Coates & Co. Cottage Sock: 14 (20, 26, 32) yards [13 (18, 24, 29) m] in Color No. 09 Gold (CC3)

Needles

US size 1 (2.25 mm)
US size 2 (2.75 mm)

Notions

Measuring tape, stitch markers (including a clasp marker), snips, tapestry needle

GAUGE

32 sts = 4" (10 cm), knit in colorwork pattern on US size 2 (2.75 mm) needles in the round and blocked

SIZES

S (M, L, XL)

MEASUREMENTS

The numbers below refer to the circumference of the ball of the foot, not the measurements of the finished sock.

7 (8, 9, 10)" [18 (20, 23, 25) cm]

PYRAMID CHART

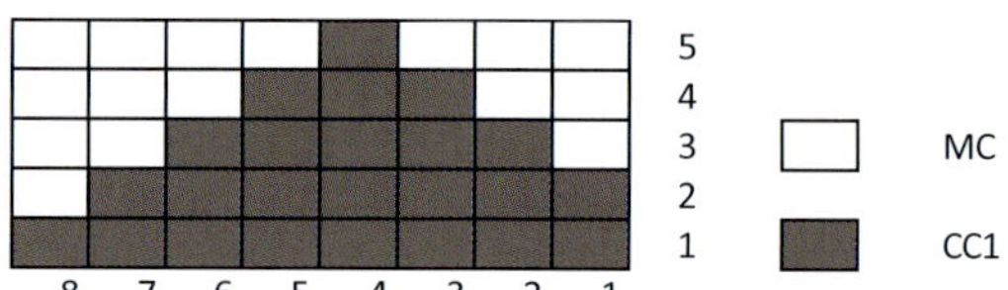

INSTRUCTIONS

Cuff

With MC and US size 1 (2.25 mm) needles, CO **57 (63, 72, 81)** sts and join for working in the rnd, being careful not to twist your sts. Est 2×1 ribbing: [k2, p1] to end.

Cont working the ribbing until your Cuff measures ¾" (2 cm), or your desired length. On the last rnd of the ribbing, we need to get our stitch count back to an even number. If you are working size **L**, you already have an even number and can move on to the Leg instructions. The rest of you, make the following increase or decrease according to your size:

S: Work in rib pattern to the last 3 sts, k2tog, p1. **56 sts.**

M: Work in rib pattern to the last 3 sts, kfb, k1, p1. **64 sts.**

XL: Work in rib pattern to the last 3 sts, k2tog, p1. **80 sts.**

Don't cut MC.

Leg

Join in CC1 and begin working the Pyramid Chart. Repeat all 5 rnds of the chart until Leg, including Cuff, measures 3½" (9 cm), or your desired length. Stop and place the waste yarn for the Heel *after* you have worked rnd 5.

Placing the Waste Yarn for the Forethought Heel

Work rnd 1 of the Pyramid Chart across the first **28 (32, 36, 40)** sts. Next, work the remaining **28 (32, 36, 40)** sts in a strand of waste yarn. Finally, transfer those **28 (32, 36, 40)** sts you just knit in your waste yarn from your right-hand needle back to your left-hand needle. Cont working rnd 4 of the chart across those waste yarn sts you just transferred back to your left needle. You have now knit a strand of waste yarn where your Forethought Heel will eventually go.

Foot

Cont repeating all 5 rnds of the chart (you should be on rnd 2 now) until your Foot reaches the desired length. The Craft Yarn Council has issued the following guidelines for the Foot of a sock, measured from the back of the Heel to the end of the Toe.

(All sizes are US.)
Women's shoe sizes 4–6.5: 8–9" (20.25–23 cm)
Women's shoe sizes 7–9.5: 9¼–10" (23.5–25.5 cm)
Women's shoe sizes 10–12.5: 10¼–11" (26–28 cm)
Men's shoe sizes 6–8.5: 9¼–10" (23.5–25.5 cm)
Men's shoe sizes 9–11.5: 10¼–11" (26–28 cm)
Men's shoe sizes 12–14: 11¼–12" (28.5–30.5 cm)

When working a Forethought Heel, you need to take into account both your Heel length and your Toe length (they will be the same).

S: 1½" (4 cm)
M: 1½" (4 cm)
L: 1½" (4 cm)
XL: 1¾" (4 cm)

Now, take your desired Foot length, from the back of the Heel to the end of the Toe, and subtract both your Heel and Toe measurements. For example, my desired Foot length is 9" (23 cm). I subtract my Toe (1½" [4 cm]) and my Heel (1½" [4 cm]) and that leaves me with 6" (15 cm) I need to knit before starting my Toe decreases.

Toes

Cut MC and CC1. With CC3 and US size 1 (2.25 mm) needles, begin the following decrease pattern for your Toes:

Rnd 1: K1, ssk, k**22 (26, 30, 34)** sts, k2tog, k1, pm, k1, ssk, k**22 (26, 30, 34)** sts, k2tog, k1.

Rnd 2: Knit.

Rnd 3: K1, ssk, knit to 3 sts before next marker, k2tog, k1, sl m, k1, ssk, knit around to 3 sts before end of rnd, k2tog, k1.

Repeat rnds 2 and 3 until **24 (28, 32, 36)** sts remain.

Graft your Toe closed using Kitchener Stitch.

Knitting the Forethought Heel

You should have a long tube with a Cuff at one end and a Toe at the other end. Go to the point in your tube where you knit in that line of waste yarn. Make sure your tube is pressed flat. You should have half your sts facing up at you and the other half of your sts facing down. Your Toe should look like a wedge, with the decrease lines on the sides of the wedge.

Identify the line of sts directly below the waste yarn. Select the first st directly below the first waste line st. With US size 1 (2.25 mm) needles, insert the tip of your needle into the right leg of that first st. Next, insert the needle into the right leg of the second st, and then into the right leg of the third st. Cont inserting your needle into the right leg of every st until you have picked up **28 (32, 36, 40)** sts. Next, repeat that process for the line of sts on the other side of the waste yarn. You should now have **56 (64, 72, 80)** sts on your needles ready to be knit.

Join in CC2 and knit 2 rnds even in Stockinette, then begin the following decrease pattern for your Heel:

Rnd 1: K1, ssk, k**22 (26, 30, 34)** sts, k2tog, k1, pm, k1, ssk, k**22 (26, 30, 34)**sts, k2tog, k1.

Rnd 2: Knit.

Rnd 3: K1, ssk, knit to 3 sts before next marker, k2tog, k1, sl m, k1, ssk, knit around to 3 sts before end of rnd, k2tog, k1.

Repeat rnds 2 and 3 until **24 (28, 32, 36)** sts remain.

Note: You can adjust the depth and fit of your Heel by working more or fewer decrease rnds. Try the sock on occasionally as you work your decreases to see how it's fitting. Stop your decreases when you can easily pinch the fabric closed.

Use Kitchener Stitch to close up your Heel.

Finishing

Weave in all your ends and block your socks.

The French Coat Socks

The Infamous French Coat

I recently purchased a billowing red and pink plaid wool coat from France. It is, to put it mildly, *outlandish*. I am not prone to wearing loud, colorful garments, and thus nearly shocked myself into a coma when I ordered it. My hand was moving completely independently of my mind, guided stubbornly by my heart's sudden intense desire to possess this ridiculous French coat (thank you Instagram ads!).

It arrived on a late summer morning, and despite the sweltering heat, I put it on immediately and then spent the day swanning about my living room in a T-shirt, athletic shorts, and The Coat. I just needed a cigarette, a pair of Chanel sunglasses, and a lithe greyhound dog, to be the picture of European eccentricity.

These socks, as you might have surmised from their name, were designed solely to be worn with The Coat. It is my favorite thing in my closet, and it needed a pair of socks that were colorful yet sophisticated to wear with it. What's more sophisticated than delicate little cables on a sock cuff paired with classic Breton stripes?!

DIFFICULTY LEVEL

Advanced beginner

SKILLS

Cable knitting
Striped knitting
Afterthought heel

MATERIALS

Yarn

Knit Picks Stroll [75% fine superwash merino/25% nylon; 230 yards (211 m); 1¾ ounces (50 g)]: 78 (94, 117, 136) yards [71 (86, 107, 124) m] in Cranberry Heather (MC)

Knit Picks Stroll: 34 (48, 57, 70) yards [31 (44, 52, 64) m] in Pucker (CC1)

Hedgehog Fibres Sock [90% superwash merino/10% nylon; 437 yards (400 m); 3½ ounces (100 g)]: 28 (34, 40, 46) yards [26 (31, 37, 42) m] in Silence (CC2)

Coates & Co. Cottage Sock [75% superwash merino/25% nylon; 437 yards (400 m); 3½ ounces (100 g)]: 28 (34, 40, 46) yards [26 (31, 37, 42) m] in Color No. 08 Bright Peach (CC3)

La Bien Aimée Super Sock [75% merino, 25% nylon; 465 yards (425 m); 3½ ounces (100 g)]: 38 (46, 54, 62) yards [35 (42, 49, 57) m] in Seaglass (CC4)

Needles

US size 1 (2.25 mm)

Notions

Tapestry needle, stitch markers (including a clasp marker), snips, measuring tape

GAUGE

32 sts = 4" (10 cm), knit in cabled rib pattern in the rnd and blocked

36 sts = 4" (10 cm), knit in Stockinette in the rnd and blocked

SIZES

S (M, L, XL)

MEASUREMENTS

The numbers below refer to the circumference of the ball of the foot, not the measurements of the finished sock.

7 (8, 9, 10)" [18 (20, 23, 25) cm]

CABLE INSTRUCTIONS

C4F (Cable 4 Front): Slip 2 sts to CN and hold to front; k2, k2 from CN.

C4B (Cable 4 Back): Slip 2 sts to CN and hold to back; k2, k2 from CN.

INSTRUCTIONS

Cuff

With CC2, CO **56 (64, 72, 80)** sts and join for working in the rnd, being careful not to twist your sts.

Setup Rnd: P1, k4, p2, [k2, p2] **4 (5, 6, 7)** times, k4, p1.

You have now established your cabled rib pattern. Begin the following cabled rib pattern repeat.

Rnds 1, 2, and 4: P1, k4, p2, [k2, p2] **4 (5, 6, 7)** times, k4, p1.

Rnd 3: P1, C4B, p2, [k2, p2] **4 (5, 6, 7)** times, C4F, p1.

Repeat these 4 rnds a total of 3 times. Cut CC2 and join in CC3. Repeat the Cable and Rib pattern 3 times, then work rnds 1 and 2. Cut CC3.

Leg

Join in MC and work 3 rnds even in Stockinette (knit every round). Begin the following stripe pattern:

2 rnds in CC1

7 rnds in MC.

Be sure to check out page 000 for helpful hints on avoiding a jog when working stripes.

Cont working the stripe pattern in Stockinette until Leg (including Cuff) measures 4½" (11 cm), or your desired length. Stop *after* working 3 rnds of a MC stripe.

Placing the Marker for the Afterthought Heel

You should be on rnd 4 of an MC stripe. To place your marker, simply knit **42 (48, 54, 60)** sts, and clip a clasp marker onto that last st you just knit. Then just keep knitting to the end of the rnd. You have now marked where your Afterthought Heel will eventually go, and you should now be ready to work rnd 5 of the MC stripe.

Foot

Cont working the stripe pattern in Stockinette until your Foot reaches the desired length. The Craft Yarn Council has issued the following guidelines for the Foot of a sock, measured from the back of the Heel to the end of the Toe.

(All sizes are US.)
Women's shoe sizes 4–6.5: 8–9" (20.25–23 cm)
Women's shoe sizes 7–9.5: 9¼–10" (23.5–25.5 cm)
Women's shoe sizes 10–12.5: 10¼–11" (26–28 cm)
Men's shoe sizes 6–8.5: 9¼–10" (23.5–25.5 cm)
Men's shoe sizes 9–11.5: 10¼–11" (26–28 cm)
Men's shoe sizes 12–14: 11¼–12" (28.5–30.5 cm)

When working an Afterthought Heel, you need to take into account both your Heel length and your Toe length (they will be the same).

S: 1½" (4 cm)
M: 1½" (4 cm)
L: 1½" (4 cm)
XL: 1¾" (4 cm)

Now, take your desired Foot length, from the back of the Heel to the end of the Toe, and subtract both your Heel and Toe measurements. For example, my desired Foot length is 9" (23 cm). I subtract my Toe (1½" [4 cm]), and my Heel (1½" [4 cm]) and that leaves me with 6" (15 cm) I need to knit before starting my Toe decreases.

Toe

Break MC and CC1 and join in CC4. Knit 1 rnd even in Stockinette, then begin the following decrease pattern to shape your Toe:

Rnd 1: K1, ssk, k**22 (26, 30, 34)** sts, k2tog, k1, pm, k1, ssk, k**22 (26, 30, 34)** sts, k2tog, k1.

Rnd 2: Knit.

Rnd 3: K1, ssk, knit to 3 sts before next marker, k2tog, k1, sl m, k1, ssk, knit around to 3 sts before end of rnd, k2tog, k1.

Repeat rnds 2 and 3 until **24 (28, 32, 36)** sts remain.

Use Kitchener Stitch to close up your Toe.

Knitting the Afterthought Heel

You should have a long tube with a Cuff at one end and a Toe at the other end. Go to the point in your tube where you placed the clasp marker. Make sure your tube is pressed flat. You should have half your sts facing up at you and the other half of your sts facing down. Your Toe should look like a wedge, with the decrease lines on the sides of the wedge.

Identify the line of sts directly below the clasp marker. Select the first st at the edge of your tube. With US size 1 (2.25 mm) needles, insert the needle into the right leg of that first st. Next, insert the needle into the right leg of the second st, and then into the right leg of the third st. Cont inserting your needle into the right leg of every st until you have picked up **28 (32, 36, 40)** sts. Next, repeat that process for the line of sts on the other side of your waste yarn. You should have **56 (64, 72, 80)** sts total divided evenly on your needles.

Remove the marker and tease that st up with your tapestry needle. Snip that st, being very careful not to snip anything else! Use your tapestry needle to tease out the yarn you've snipped from the sts. Start in the middle and go to the end on either side of your snipped st.

You now have a gaping hole in your sock tube and live Heel sts on the needles, ready to be worked. You also have a strand of yarn dangling on each side of the hole. Those will come in handy later when you weave in your ends. I use them to close gaps at the corners of the Heel.

Join in CC4 and knit 2 rnds even in Stockinette, then begin the following decrease pattern for your Heel:

Rnd 1: K1, ssk, k**22 (26, 30, 34)** sts, k2tog, k1, pm, k1, ssk, k**22 (26, 30, 34)** sts, k2tog, k1.

Rnd 2: Knit.

Rnd 3: K1, ssk, knit to 3 sts before next marker, k2tog, k1, sl m, k1, ssk, knit around to 3 sts before end of rnd, k2tog, k1.

Repeat rnds 2 and 3 until **24 (28, 32, 36)** sts remain.

Note: You can adjust the depth and fit of your Heel by working more or fewer decrease rnds. Try the sock on occasionally as you work your decreases to see how it's fitting. Stop your decreases when you can easily pinch the fabric closed.

Use Kitchener Stitch to close up your Heel.

Finishing

Weave in all your ends and block your socks.

Subtle Block Socks

Going on adventures with my family always inspires new design ideas. This is us in Sedona, Arizona, after climbing up Bell Rock.

I frequently get asked what inspires me. What a question! How do I even begin to answer that when inspiration comes from everywhere and everything, all the time, all at once? Memories, feelings, colors flashing by as I whiz down the road, songs, snippets of books, moods and emotions, fragments of everyday life embedded deep in my soul that pop out unexpectedly when I smell a certain laundry detergent or hear someone laugh a certain way? And then trying to translate those ephemeral bits of flotsam into a knitted sock? It would be much easier if I were skilled at drawing or painting.

Some socks, however, come about solely because a certain color combination caught my eye in my stash. There is no deeper, complex meaning in the stitches, just a simple joy over how good two colors look together. The next step is finding a stitch pattern that will be interesting to knit and that will allow the colors to shine.

The Subtle Block Socks are the ones you knit when all you want is a simple but engaging pattern that will allow your color choices to pop. The texture winks through, adding just enough interest to complement the palette you choose. I've been eyeing this neon green and soft lavender combination in my stash for quite some time, but I'm also tempted to knit these up in a speckled yarn.

DIFFICULTY LEVEL

Beginner

SKILLS

Heel flap and gusset

MATERIALS

Yarn

Cascade Heritage [75% superwash merino/ 25% nylon; 437 yards (400 m); 3½ ounces (100 g)]: (126) 142 (169, 194, 221) yards [(115) 130 (155, 177, 202) m] in 5779 Thistle (MC)

La Bien Aimée Super Sock [75% merino/ 25% nylon; 465 yards (425 m); 3½ ounces (100 g)]: (30) 38 (46, 54, 62) yards [(27) 35 (42, 49, 57) m] in Ecto 1 (CC)

Needles

US size 1 (2.25 mm)

Notions

Measuring tape, stitch markers, snips, tapestry needle

GAUGE

32 sts = 4" (10 cm), knit in Basket Weave Pattern in the rnd and blocked

SIZES

(Kid) S (M, L, XL)

MEASUREMENTS

The numbers below refer to the circumference of the ball of the foot, not the measurements of the finished sock.

(5–6) 7 (8, 9, 10)" [(13–15) 18 (20, 23, 25) cm]

BASKETWEAVE PATTERN

Rnds 1–7: [K4, p4] to end.
Rnds 8–14: [P4, k4] to end.

INSTRUCTIONS

Cuff

With CC, CO **(48) 56 (64, 72, 80)** sts and join for working in the rnd, being careful not to twist your sts. Est 1×1 rib pattern: [k1, p1] to end.

Cont in 1×1 rib pattern until Cuff measures 2" (5 cm), or your desired length.

Cut CC.

Leg

Join in MC and begin working Basketweave Pattern. Repeat all 14 rnds of the pattern until Leg (including Cuff) measures 5" (13 cm), or your desired length. You can stop at any point in the Basketweave Pattern.

Heel Flap

Work in Basketweave Pattern across the first **(24) 28 (32, 36, 40)** sts, then begin working your Heel Flap back and forth across the remaining **(24) 28 (32, 36, 40)** sts as follows:

Row 1 (RS): K2, [slip 1, k1] to end. Turn work.

Row 2 (WS): Slip 1 wyif, purl to end. Turn work.

Row 3: [Slip 1, k1] to end. Turn work.

Repeat rows 2 and 3 until Heel Flap measures **(1¾) 2 (2, 2¼, 2½)" [(4) 5 (5, 6, 6.5) cm]**. End *after* you have worked row 3.

Heel Turn

Row 1 (WS): Slip 1 wyif, p**(12) 14 (16, 18, 20)**, p2tog, p1, turn.

Row 2 (RS): Slip 1, k3, ssk, k1, turn.

Row 3: Slip 1 wyif, p4, p2tog, p1, turn.

Row 4: Slip 1, k5, ssk, k1, turn.

You have now established the following pattern for your Heel Turn: Slip 1, knit or purl to 1 st before the gap created by turning on the previous row, ssk or p2tog, k1 or p1, turn. Cont in this pattern until all your Heel sts have been worked, ending on a RS row. You should now have **(14) 16 (18, 20, 22)** Heel sts.

Gusset

With the right side of your work facing, pick up and knit **(10) 12 (14, 16, 18)** sts along the left side of your Heel Flap.

Next, work in Basketweave Pattern across the **(24) 28 (32, 36, 40)** sts that we've left undisturbed on our needles while working our Heel Flap. Pm, and pick up **(10) 12 (14, 16, 18)** sts on the right side of the Heel Flap. Knit across the Heel sts, then knit down the first set of new sts you picked up on the left side. You've reached the end of the rnd, and all your sts have now been picked up. You should now have **(58) 68 (78, 88, 98)** sts on your needles.

Gusset Decreases

Rnd 1: Work in Basketweave Pattern across **(24) 28 (32, 36, 40)** sts, sl m, k1, ssk, knit around to 3 sts before the end of rnd, k2tog, k1.

Rnd 2: Work even with no decreases.

Repeat these 2 rnds until you have **(48) 56 (64, 72, 80)** sts on your needles.

Foot

Cont working in Basketweave Pattern across the first **(24) 28 (32, 36, 40)** sts and in Stockinette across the remaining **(24) 28 (32, 36, 40)** sts until your Foot reaches just to the tip of your pinky toe. If you can't easily try on your socks as you knit (working on double-pointed needles or tiny circulars can make this challenging), or if you are knitting gift socks for some lucky recipient, the Craft Yarn Council has issued the following length guidelines for the Foot of a sock, measured from the back of the Heel to the end of the Toe.

(All sizes are US.)
Kid: 6–7½" (15–19 cm)
Women's shoe sizes 4–6.5: 8–9" (20.25–23 cm)
Women's shoe sizes 7–9.5: 9¼–10" (23.5–25.5 cm)
Women's shoe sizes 10–12.5: 10¼–11" (26–28 cm)
Men's shoe sizes 6–8.5: 9¼–10" (23.5–25.5 cm)
Men's shoe sizes 9–11.5: 10¼–11" (26–28 cm)
Men's shoe sizes 12–14: 11¼–12" (28.5–30.5 cm)

When working a Heel Flap and Gusset, you need to take into account your Toe length.

Kid: 1¼" (3 cm)
S: 1½" (4 cm)
M: 1½" (4 cm)
L: 1½" (4 cm)
XL: 1¾" (4 cm)

Now, take your desired Foot length, from the back of the Heel to the end of the Toe, and subtract your Toe measurement. For example, my desired Foot length is 9" (23 cm). I subtract my Toe (1½" [4 cm]) and that leaves me with 7½" (19 cm) I need to knit before starting my Toe decreases. Measure starting at the back of the Heel.

Toe

Cut MC and join in CC. Work 1 rnd even, then begin the following decrease pattern for your Toes:

Rnd 1: K1, ssk, k**(18) 22 (26, 30, 34)** sts, k2tog, k1, pm, k1, ssk, k**(18) 22 (26, 30, 34)** sts, k2tog, k1.

Rnd 2: Knit.

Rnd 3: K1, ssk, knit to 3 sts before next marker, k2tog, k1, sl m, k1, ssk, knit around to 3 sts before end of rnd, k2tog, k1.

Repeat rnds 2 and 3 until **(20) 24 (28, 32, 36)** sts remain.

Use Kitchener Stitch to close up your Toe.

Finishing

Weave in all your ends and block your socks.

Nordic Brights Socks

If ever there was a sock that fully expressed who I am, it's this one. Simple Scandinavian motifs that are easy to knit? Yes please! Bright happy colors combined in both harmonious and surprising ways? Absolutely! An overall vibe of cheer, comfort, and coziness? It's all there! Friends, I adore these socks, and so I saved them for last. What better way to close out this book than with the socks I had the most fun knitting, and the most fun staring at long after they were done.

They may look complicated to knit, but fear not. The motifs truly are easy to work. You only ever work with two colors at once, and the repeats are simple to follow. I chose to use many (many, many) colors for mine, but you could knit the entire sock in just two colors if you want. Further, you don't have to use all the included charts. Repeat the same chart all the way down or pick two or three to repeat—it's totally up to you!

If you go my route with lots of colors, you might want to stop occasionally to weave in your ends. Your future self will be so grateful that you took a few minutes here and there to keep those ends under control. There's no getting around it with my colorful version—you'll have ends for days. But the final sock makes it so worth it.

DIFFICULTY LEVEL

Intermediate

SKILLS

Stranded colorwork
Forethought heel

MATERIALS

Yarn

Lang Jawoll [75% virgin superwash wool/ 25% nylon; 230 yards (210 m); 1¾ ounces (50 g)]: 38 (47, 59, 68) yards [35 (43, 54, 62) m] in 94 Pearl (MC)

Once again, I dove into my scrap basket for all kinds of colorful odds and ends. You'll need an assortment of your favorites (or just two of your favorite colors) in the following total amounts for the body of your sock: 152 (174, 198, 225) yards [139 (159, 181, 206) m]

Needles

US size 1 (2.25 mm)
US size 2 (2.75 mm)

Notions

Measuring tape, stitch markers (including a clasp marker), snips, tapestry needle

GAUGE

32 sts = 4" (10 cm), knit in colorwork pattern on US size 2 (2.75 mm) needles in the round and blocked

SIZES

S (M, L, XL)

MEASUREMENTS

The numbers below refer to the circumference of the ball of the foot, not the measurements of the finished sock.

7 (8, 9, 10)" [18 (20, 23, 25) cm]

NORDIC BRIGHTS CHARTS

I worked these charts in the order they are listed. I started with Chart A and worked my way down through Chart H. Then I started over and kept working them in order until my sock was finished.

A

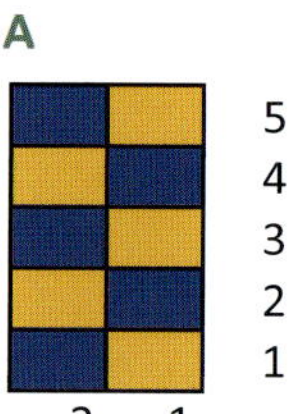

B

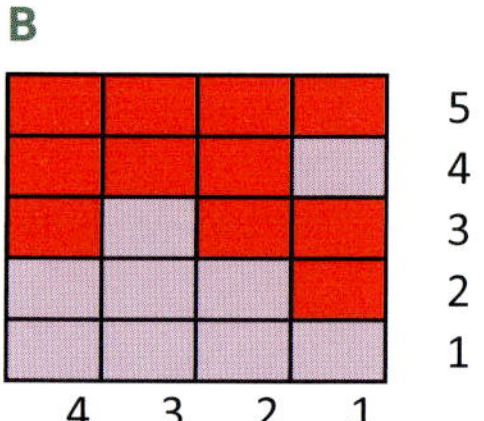

C

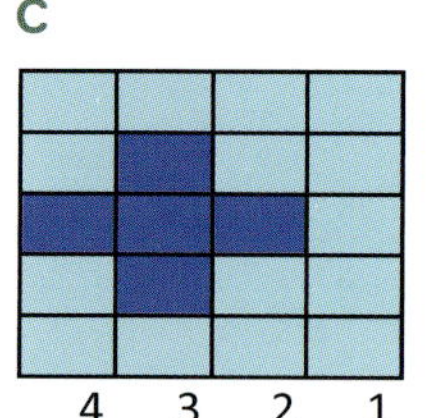

D

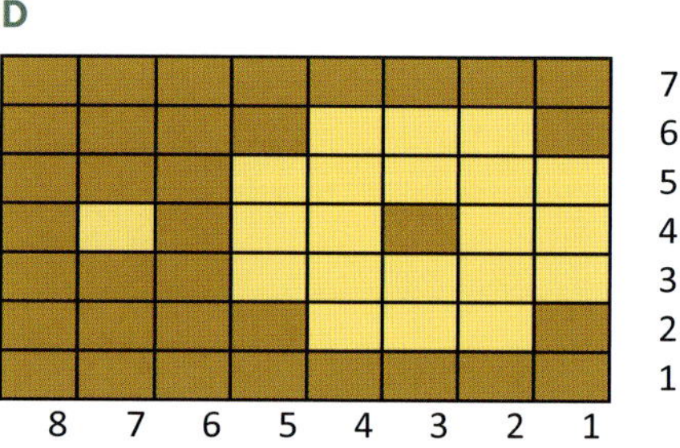

E

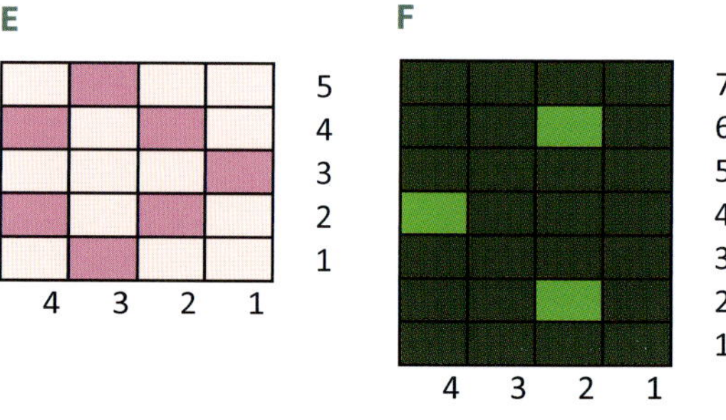

F

G

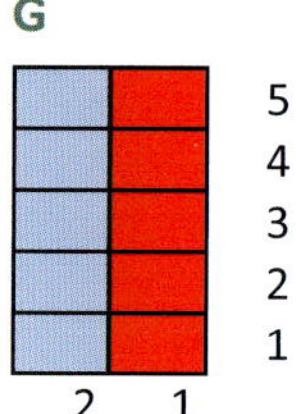

H

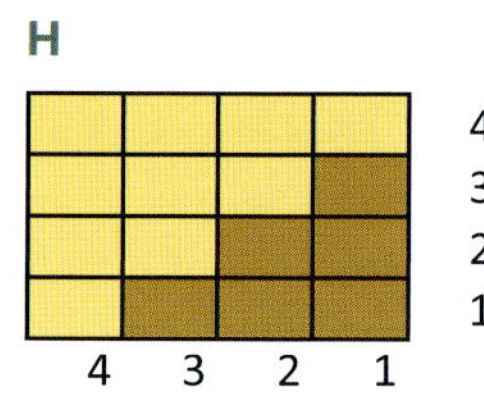

INSTRUCTIONS

Cuff

With MC and US size 1 (2.25 mm) needles, CO **57 (63, 72, 81)** sts and join for working in the rnd, being careful not to twist your sts. Est 2×1 ribbing: [k2, p1] to end.

Cont working the ribbing until your Cuff measures ¾" (2 cm), or your desired length. On the last rnd of the ribbing, we need to get our stitch count back to an even number. If you are working size **L**, you already have an even number and can move on to the Leg instructions. The rest of you, make the following increase or decrease according to your size:

S: Work in rib pattern to the last 3 sts, k2tog, p1. **56 sts.**

M: Work in rib pattern to the last 3 sts, kfb, k1, p1. **64 sts.**

XL: Work in rib pattern to the last 3 sts, k2tog, p1. **80 sts.**

Cut MC.

Leg

Join in your first two colors and begin working Chart A. Work all 5 rnds of Chart A once. Cut your colors (unless you are working the two-color only option) and join in your next two colors. Work Chart B, then cut your colors and move on to Chart C. Cont working all the rnds of each chart, changing your colors with each chart, until you have finished working Chart G.

Placing the Waste Yarn for the Forethought Heel

Work rnd 1 of Chart H across the first **28 (32, 36, 40)** sts. Next, work the remaining **28 (32, 36, 40)** sts in a strand of waste yarn. Finally, transfer those **28 (32, 36, 40)** sts you just knit in your waste yarn from your right-hand needle back to your left-hand needle. Cont working rnd 1 of Chart H across those waste yarn sts you just transferred back to your left needle. You have now knit a strand of waste yarn where your Forethought Heel will eventually go.

Foot

Work the remaining 3 rnds of Chart H, then start over at Chart A, working all charts in order again until your Foot reaches the desired length. The Craft Yarn Council has issued the following guidelines for the Foot of a sock, measured from the back of the Heel to the end of the Toe.

(All sizes are US.)
Women's shoe sizes 4–6.5: 8–9" (20.25–23 cm)
Women's shoe sizes 7–9.5: 9¼–10" (23.5–25.5 cm)
Women's shoe sizes 10–12.5: 10¼–11" (26–28 cm)
Men's shoe sizes 6–8.5: 9¼–10" (23.5–25.5 cm)
Men's shoe sizes 9–11.5: 10¼–11" (26–28 cm)
Men's shoe sizes 12–14: 11¼–12" (28.5–30.5 cm)

When working a Forethought Heel, you need to take into account both your Heel length and your Toe length (they will be the same).

S: 1½" (4 cm)
M: 1½" (4 cm)
L: 1½" (4 cm)
XL: 1¾" (4 cm)

Now, take your desired Foot length, from the back of the Heel to the end of the Toe, and subtract both your Heel and Toe measurements. For example, my desired Foot length is 9" (23 cm). I subtract my Toe (1½" [4 cm]), and my Heel (1½" [4 cm]) and that leaves me with 6" (15 cm) I need to knit before starting my Toe decreases.

Toes

Cut your colors from the last chart you worked and join in MC. Switch to US size 1 (2.25 mm) needles and work 1 rnd even before beginning the following decrease pattern for your Toes:

Rnd 1: K1, ssk, k**22 (26, 30, 34)** sts, k2tog, k1, pm, k1, ssk, k**22 (26, 30, 34)** sts, k2tog, k1.

Rnd 2: Knit.

Rnd 3: K1, ssk, knit to 3 sts before next marker, k2tog, k1, sl m, k1, ssk, knit around to 3 sts before end of rnd, k2tog, k1.

Repeat rnds 2 and 3 until **24 (28, 32, 36)** sts remain.

Graft your Toe closed using Kitchener Stitch.

Knitting the Forethought Heel

You should have a long tube with a Cuff at one end and a Toe at the other end. Go to the point in your tube where you knit in that line of waste yarn. Make sure your tube is pressed flat. You should have half your sts facing up at you, and the other half of your sts facing down. Your Toe should look like a wedge, with the decrease lines on the sides of the wedge.

Identify the line of sts directly below the waste yarn. Select the first st directly below the first waste line st. With US size 1 (2.25 mm) needles, insert the tip of your needle into the right leg of that first st. Next, insert the needle into the right leg of the second st, and then into the right leg of the third st. Cont inserting your needle into the right leg of every st until you have picked up **28 (32, 36, 40)** sts. Next, repeat that process for the line of sts on the other side of the waste yarn. You should now have **56 (64, 72, 80)** sts on your needles ready to be knit.

Join in MC and knit 2 rnds even in Stockinette, then begin the following decrease pattern for your Heel:

Rnd 1: K1, ssk, k**22 (26, 30, 34)** sts, k2tog, k1, pm, k1, ssk, k**22 (26, 30, 34)** sts, k2tog, k1.

Rnd 2: Knit.

Rnd 3: K1, ssk, knit to 3 sts before next marker, k2tog, k1, sl m, k1, ssk, knit around to 3 sts before end of rnd, k2tog, k1.

Repeat rnds 2 and 3 until **24 (28, 32, 36)** sts remain.

Note: You can adjust the depth and fit of your Heel by working more or fewer decrease rnds. Try the sock on occasionally as you work your decreases to see how it's fitting. Stop your decreases when you can easily pinch the fabric closed.

Use Kitchener Stitch to close up your Heel.

Finishing

Weave in all your ends and block your socks.

Acknowledgments

Without you, I wouldn't have the opportunity to share my love of sock knitting with the world. Your support, kind messages, pattern and book purchases, and engagement with the little community I've created online mean so much! I am forever grateful that you would choose to spend your time and hard-earned money with me.

I would also like to thank my wonderful editor, Shawna Mullen. Putting together a book like this is an all-consuming project, and Shawna provided nothing but encouragement and support the MANY times I struggled!

The entire team at Abrams Books is a dream. I couldn't be luckier to have found a home with this publisher. From copyediting to design, this group of talented people work so hard to turn a manuscript into a beautiful book that perfectly captures who I am.

My family also deserves many thanks! My husband, Dave, steps up without complaint and takes on everything while I hole up writing and knitting. My two teens, Memphis and Sailor, keep me in good spirits by sharing all the good high school gossip and making me laugh with their funny observations on everything.

Finally, I would like to thank my sweet Grandma Mae, who passed away earlier this year. She was a deep well of love and support from my earliest memories. She read *Petunia* and *Charlotte's Web* to me as a kid, sparking a lifelong love of reading and writing. She always made me feel loved and special, and I will forever be grateful for the safety and warmth I felt when I was with her.

Editor: Shawna Mullen
Designer: Jenice Kim
Managing Editor: Lisa Silverman
Production Manager: Sarah Masterson Hally

Library of Congress Control Number: 2025941986

ISBN: 978-1-4197-8046-2
eISBN: 979-8-88707-621-8

Printed and bound in China
10 9 8 7 6 5 4 3 2 1

ABRAMS is represented in the UK and Europe by Abrams & Chronicle Books, 1 West Smithfield, London EC1A 9JU and Média-Participations, 57 rue Gaston Tessier, 75166 Paris, France.
abramsandchronicle.co.uk and media-participations.com
info@abramsandchronicle.co.uk

ABRAMS The Art of Books
195 Broadway, New York, NY 10007
abramsbooks.com